Islamic Studies

Level 6

Mansur Ahmad, Husain A. Nuri

Weekend Learning

ISBN 10: 0-9791916-6-1
ISBN 13: 978-0-9791916-6-4

First edition: 2008

Cover Design and Photography: Mansur Ahmad
Illustrations: Mansur Ahmad, Husain A. Nuri

WeekendLearning Publishers
5584 Boulder Crest St
Columbus, OH 43235
www.weekendlearning.com

Printed in the United States of America

Preface

The concept of a series of Islamic Studies books was conceived in 2002 when both of us were teachers and/or principals of two weekend schools in two different states. We used several excellent textbooks or reference books for the schools. However, as teachers soon we realized there were no single textbook available that could meet our classroom needs. Some of the available books have too many or too few lessons for an academic year. Some lessons are too long for a class hour, some are too short. Some lessons are too difficult for the age; some are too basic for higher classes. Some books are written without a 12 year curriculum in mind. The lessons in higher grades, therefore, did not develop from the knowledge base of the prior years. Sometimes, extra emphasis was placed on one topic at the cost of other important topics. We thought a balanced knowledge base was, thus, lost.

We always felt there ought to be a way out. We began writing the lessons ourselves to meet the needs of our schools. We involved other teachers. For the next two years, we conducted classes based on the lessons we prepared. In the meantime, both of us met other principals and teachers across the country. We wanted to find out how they teach Islamic Studies and what their major concerns were. Most of the principals and teachers we talked to, expressed their inability to find or develop a good curriculum. If they had a curriculum they could not find lessons to complement the curriculum.

This survey prompted us to develop a functional, comprehensive curriculum for weekend schools in the West. We wanted to have a curriculum that would include everything Muslim students growing up in the West would ideally need to know. We wanted to include topics based on the life experiences of students growing up in the West. Muslim children growing up in the US, Europe and Australia are facing diverse challenges and conflicting pressures at schools and at friend circles. They are constantly influenced by mainstream youth culture. We wanted lessons to address their issues from their perspective.

The curriculum alone would not be of any use unless there were lessons based on the curriculum. The lessons had to be age appropriate, suitable for typical class duration of most of the schools. As we continued to write and edit lessons over the next two years, we made the curriculum increasingly meaningful.

In 2007 we published pre-printed coil bound versions of these books. More than thirty schools in the US and UK used the books. We also received large number of inquiries from many other schools. Based on the suggestions, comments and reviews received from many of these schools, we have edited the books and made changes as appropriate.

We are thankful to Allāh for giving us the ability to write these books. We pray to Allāh to accept our labor and make us successful in communicating the message of Islam. We hope Islamic schools and home schools in the USA and other countries will find these books useful. Any mistakes or errors in the books are our fault. We will appreciate receiving meaningful comments and suggestions to improve the series.

"Our Rabb! Accept from us, you indeed are the all-Hearing, all-Knowing." (2:127)

January 15, 2008

Mansur Ahmad
Husain A. Nuri

Table of Contents

How to use this book effectively
For The Teacher and The Parents

The lessons for sixth grade Islamic Studies expand from the key information on Islam learned in the previous years. As with other books in the series, this book, too, starts with a few topics on Allāh (swt). Different aspects of the Qur'an are discussed in three different lessons. Apart from some of the prophets, the lives of 'Ā'ishah (ra) and Fātimah (ra) are discussed. Some related **Interesting Facts** and **Points to Remember** are included in some lessons to impart knowledge about the creations of Allāh, and also to make a connection between the *deen* and the *dunya*. Islamic views on dating and inter-gender mixing is discussed this year. Similar topics and issues will be discussed in the upcoming years.

For maximum benefit, each lesson should be completed in one class hour. We recommend that a test be conducted after every fifth or sixth lesson. Weekend Learning has designed an Excel based user friendly program to record homework and exam scores. It will become handy when report cards are prepared. For this program as well as question bank, ready to print exam and homework questions obtain a CD from the publisher.

Homework:

Teachers are requested to assign regular homework, and also grade them regularly. For this grade, the time commitment for homework is about 10-15 minutes per lesson. It is strongly encouraged that parents supervise the student for the homework. A regular supervision of homework by a parent will indicate that the education is valued.

Regular interaction with the Qur'ān:

Every Muslim student should develop the habit of interacting with the Qur'ān on a regular basis. To complete some homework, an acceptable English translation of the Qur'ān is strongly recommended. The purpose of such homework is to build a strong connection between the student and the Qur'ān. Insha-Allāh, such homework will put a seed in the minds of the children to continue lifelong interaction with the Qur'ān.

Teaching Respect:

From an early age, students should be taught to show respect to Allāh, His Prophets and Angels. The teachers and parents are requested to mention the following:

Whenever the word Allāh appears in the book, please add the glorification "Subhāna-hu wa-Ta'ālā."

Whenever the word Muhammad, or other words indicating Muhammad, e.g. Rasulullah, the Prophet, or Nabi appears, please add the prayer, "Salla-llāhu 'alaihi wa Sallam." We have used (S) in the book to remind the prayer. Whenever the student comes across the names of a prophet or an angel, please add the prayer "Alai-hi-s Salām". This is noted by (A). The students should be taught to add the prayer "Radi-allāhu 'an-hu" for a khalifa or a male companion of the Prophet (S). For a woman companion, the prayer "Radi-allāhu 'an-hā" should be used. These are noted by (R) or (ra).

Suggestions:

Please provide suggestions, corrections, ideas, etc., to improve the book by sending an e-mail to the publisher at weekendLearning@gmail.com. It is a combined effort of the publisher, authors, teachers and parents to prepare our future ummah. May Allāh guide us all. Amin.

Attributes of Allāh: *These Are The Most Beautiful*

Objective of the Lesson:

Attributes or qualities of Allāh are endless. By understanding the attributes we can get a good comprehension about Allāh. If we understand these qualities, it will be easier for us to submit completely to Him. This introductory lesson discusses some of the attributes of Allāh, and sets the pace for the rest of the chapters in the school year.

We know Allāh is our God. He is the God of the entire world. We worship Him. We have to read the Qur'ān to know more about who Allāh is and what He does. The Qur'ān is Allāh's word. One way to learn about Allāh is to learn His names, which are the most beautiful names.[7:180; 17:110] In Arabic, these beautiful names are called **al-Asmā al-husnā**. We are not only going to memorize these names, but we shall also apply some of the beautiful qualities in our behavior.

Why the most beautiful names: In the Qur'ān, Allāh mentioned more than 99 of His names. All these names describe something about Allāh. These names are said to be beautiful because the names express Allāh's qualities. We can never measure Allāh's qualities. We can only try to understand a part of His endless qualities.

In the list of Allāh's beautiful names, you will never find bad names. You will never find a name of Allāh, such as most-Rude, most-Cruel, most-Jealous, etc. You will also never find any Muslim mention Allāh as the "father" like the Christians address their god.

Understanding the beautiful names: Allāh's names tell us about His attributes and essence. Attribute means the inner quality of something or someone. Essence means most significant content of something. Allāh's two beautiful names are most-Kind and most-Generous. Among the human beings, we may have a person who is kind and generous. For example, we may say Miriam or Abdullah is kind and generous, but Akram's father is more kind and generous than Miriam or Abdullah. There may be someone else who is even more kind and generous than Akram's father. However, nobody is more kind or more generous than Allāh. All the beautiful names of Allāh tell us nobody is more beautiful or has more qualities than Allāh.

Let us learn a few names of Allāh (swt) with their meanings.

Rabb: One of Allāh's names is Rabb. The word Rabb is often translated in English as the Lord, but this choice of word does not tell us enough about Rabb. A simple literal meaning of this word is "One who nourishes." Allāh (swt) not only provides and nourishes this universe, He also makes this universe mature and progress. In the very first verse of sūrah Al-Fātihah, Allāh (swt) introduces Himself as the Rabb of all the worlds (*rabb-il 'alamīn*). He is not only the owner of the universe, but He is also responsible for its growth.

Ar-Rahman — the most-Kind: The second verse of sūrah Al-Fātihah points out two other qualities of Allāh (swt)—**Ar-Rahman** and **Ar-Rahim**. Both names originate from the same root word; they are similar yet quite different. Ar-Rahman is the word that tells Allāh (swt) is the most-Kind or the most-Gracious. This quality of Allāh (swt) tells us that He will give us things without any effort on our part. We do not have to work extra to earn some

fresh air. There are many things in this world that we take for granted. All these exist just because Allāh (swt) is the most-Kind. The solid ground under our feet is a blessing from Allāh (swt). We did not do anything extra to earn this ground. He gave us sunshine, and He gave us air to breathe. We did not ask for these, and we did nothing to enjoy these. Yet Allāh (swt) gave these gifts to us

without limit. He is not partial with these gifts. He freely gives these gifts to both the righteous as well as the sinner. He sent these gifts for us even before we were born. For our spiritual growth, He even sent us rasuls to show us the Right Path.

Ar-Rahim — the most-Merciful: Although the word Ar-Rahim is quite similar to Ar-Rahman, the literal meaning of Ar-Rahim is most Merciful or most-Rewarding. A reward is not a gift. While a reward is earned, a gift is given to a recipient who puts no extra effort. Allāh (swt) rewards us for every good deed that we do. Allāh (swt) gives some rewards in this world, and will give more rewards in the

Hereafter. The amount of rewards is based on our good deeds. The result of doing a bad deed is punishment. Since Allāh (swt) is Ar-Rahim, His punishment is equal to the amount of the sin, but His reward is many times more than the good work.[6:160] If we repent Allāh (swt) may forgive our sin altogether.[39:53] However, He never ignores a good deed.[21:47, 31:16]

Malik—the Master: Another important name of Allāh (swt) is al-Malik or the King. It also means the Sovereign Lord or the Absolute Ruler. Allāh (swt) has complete Dominion over the entire creation.

Other Names: In this class we cannot finish describing each and every beautiful name of Allāh. But here is a short summary.

Al-Fattāh is a qualitative name of Allāh (swt) which means that He opens

the gates of success and removes the darkness from our minds. Another name is **Al-'Adl**, which means He is Just. A good judge will reward the righteous and punish the evil. Only an inferior judge will ignore to punish the evil ones. Allāh is the best Judge, and because He knows everything, He is **Al-'Alīm**. We cannot hide anything from Him. He knows about every leaf that falls from a tree. No one can change evidence in His Court, since He sees all, He is **Al-Basīr**, and He hears all things, He is **As-Sāmi**.

Some religions say that their god is all-Loving and all-Forgiving. A judge who loves everyone and forgives everyone is in fact an unfit judge. You can never expect to get justice from such a judge. Forgiving a crime is unfair not only for the victim but also for the criminal. A good gardener regularly trims his plants and removes the weed.

A good parent sometimes disciplines their child because through discipline, the child comes to know the good from the bad. Allāh punishes us for our bad deeds and rewards us for our good deeds. Allāh is the most-Loving (**Al-Wadūd**) and the most forgiving (**Al-Ghaffar**) but He is also the Supreme Judge at the same time.

Limitless Qualities of Allāh (swt): We cannot finish counting the qualities, attributes or essence of Allāh (swt). We cannot fully describe the qualities of Allāh (swt).[6:103] There is nothing that is similar to Him.[42:11] We should try to memorize as many of Allāh's beautiful names as we can and then try to apply the beautiful qualities in our own lives.

$$قُلِ ٱدْعُوا۟ ٱللَّهَ أَوِ ٱدْعُوا۟ ٱلرَّحْمَٰنَ أَيًّا مَّا تَدْعُوا۟ فَلَهُ ٱلْأَسْمَآءُ ٱلْحُسْنَىٰ$$

Say: "Call upon as Allāh or call upon as Rahman. By whatever you call, His are then the most beautiful names..." (Bani Isra'il 17:110)

99 Beautiful Names of Allāh

Allāh	Allāh	Al-Wahhāb	The Giver of All
Ar-Rahman	The most-Kind	Ar-Razzāq	The Sustainer
Ar-Rahīm	The most-Rewarding	Al-Fattāh	The Opener
Al-Malik	The Absolute Ruler	Al-'Alīm	The Knower of All
Al-Quddūs	The Pure One	Al-Qābid	The Constrictor
As-Salām	The Source of Peace	Al-Bāsit	The Reliever
Al-Mu'min	The Inspirer of Faith	Al-Khāfid	The Abaser
Al-Muhaymin	The Guardian	Ar-Rāfi'e	The Exalter
Al-'Azīz	The Victorious	Al-Mu'izz	The Bestower of Honors
Al-Jabbār	The Compeller	Al-Mudhill	The Humiliator
Al-Mutakabbīr	The Greatest	As-Sami'i	The Hearer of All
Al-Khāliq	The Creator	Al-Basīr	The Seer of All
Al-Bāri'	The Maker of Order	Al-Hakam	The Judge
Al-Musawwir	The Shaper of Beauty	Al-'Adl	The Just
Al-Ghaffār	The Forgiving	Al-Latīf	The Subtle One
Al-Qahhār	The Subduer	Al-Khabīr	The All-Aware

Al-Halīm	The Forbearing	Al-Ahad	The One
Al-'Azīm	The Magnificent	As-Samad	The Satisfier of All Needs
Al-Ghafūr	The Forgiver	Al-Qādir	The All Powerful
Ash-Shakūr	The Appreciative	Al-Muqtadir	The Creator of All Power
Al-'Ali	The Highest	Al-Muqaddim	The Expediter
Al-Kabīr	The Greatest	Al-Mu'akhkhir	The Delayer
Al-Hafīz	The Preserver	Al-Awwal	The First
Al-Muqīt	The Nourisher	Al-Akhir	The Last
Al-Hasīb	The Accounter	Az-Zāhir	The Manifest One
Al-Jalīl	The Mighty	Al-Bātin	The Hidden One
Al-Karīm	The Generous	Al-Wāli	The Protecting Friend
Ar-Raqīb	The Watchful One	Al-Muta'āli	The Supreme One
Al-Mujīb	The Responder to Prayer	Al-Barr	The Doer of Good
Al-Wāsi'i	The All-Comprehending	At-Tawwāb	The Guide to Repentance
Al-Hakīm	The Perfectly Wise	Al-Muntaqim	The Avenger
Al-Wadūd	The Loving One	Al-'Afūw	The Forgiver
Al-Majīd	The Majestic One	Ar-Ra'uf	The Clement
Al-Bā'ith	The Resurrector	Mālik al-Mulk	The Owner of All
Ash-Shahīd	The Witness	Dhul-Jalāli	The Lord of Majesty
Al-Haqq	The Truth	Wal-Ikrām	
Al-Wakīl	The Trustee	Al-Muqsīt	The Equitable One
Al-Qawi'	The Possessor of All Strength	Al-Jāmi	The Gatherer
Al-Matīn	The Forceful One	Al-Ghanī	The Rich One
Al-Wali	The Governor	Al-Mughnī	The Enricher
Al-Hamīd	The Praised One	Al-Māni'i	The Preventer of Harm
Al-Muhsī	The Appraiser	Ad-Dārr	The Creator of The Harmful
Al-Mubdī'	The Originator		
Al-Mu'īd	The Restorer	An-Nāfi'i	The Creator of Good
Al-Muhyī	The Giver of Life	An-Nūr	The Light
Al-Mumīt	The Taker of Life	Al-Hādi	The Guide
Al-Hayy	The Ever Living One	Al-Badī'	The Originator
Al-Qayyum	The Self-Existing One	Al-Bāqī	The Everlasting One
Al-Wājid	The Finder	Al-Wārith	The Inheritor of All
Al-Mājid	The Glorious	Ar-Rashīd	The Righteous Teacher
Al-Wāhid	The Only One	As-Sabūr	The Patient One

homework**weekend 1**

1. What kind of names do not belong to Allāh?

_____

2. What is the Arabic word for "most-beautiful names"—a term used to describe all of Allāh's names?

    (a)   Asma al-Allāh
    (b)   Asma al-Husna
    (c)   Asma al-Qur'ān
    (d)   Asma al-Rasul

3. Read the first four verses of sūrah Fātiha in Arabic or its translation. Then mention how many beautiful names of Allāh are mentioned in these four verses.

_____

4. See the list of 99 names of Allāh given in the chapter. From the list identify three names that start with the following letters:

starting with the letter "K" al-_____ al-_____ al-_____

starting with the letter "J" al-_____ al-_____ al-_____

starting with the letter "W" al-_____ al-_____ al-_____

5. Read the meaning of ar-Rahman. Then think and write three things that Allāh gives us without any effort on our part.

    (a)   _____

    (b)   _____

    (c)   _____

Promise of Allāh: *It is Always True*

Objective of the Lesson:

A promise is a contract between two parties. Allāh (swt) made many promises to human beings. This lesson discusses some of these promises. It also discusses our roles in fulfilling these promises. The lesson cites an incident from Mūsā (A)'s life showing that the promise of Allāh (swt) is always true. Students will also memorize one du'ā from the Qur'ān.

All of us make promises—we say we will or will not do something. We promise to ourselves, we promise to parents, friends, or to our teachers. Sometimes we keep the promise, and sometimes we promise without meaning it, therefore we do not keep the promise. In other words, we make a promise and we break it.

A promise is a two-way contract between two individuals where one person agrees to do or not do some service or give something to the other person. It may sound strange to you, but Allāh also makes promises. His promise is with us. Just like all promises involve at least two parties, Allāh's promise includes two beings—on one side is Allāh, on the other side is us, the human beings. Unlike human promises that we make and sometimes break, Allāh never breaks His promises.

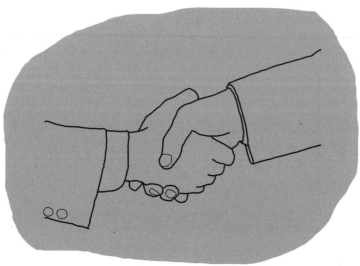

Allāh's promise in the Qur'ān: Allāh made several promises to the mankind. Allāh promised a reward of paradise to all those who believe and do good work.[4:122] He promises to protect such believers.[5:9] He also promised that the punishment for the hypocrites and unbelievers will be in the hellfire.[9:68] People in paradise and those in hell, will realize that the promises of Allāh came true.[7:44] Whatever Allāh promises, He will fulfill it. It is His obligation to fulfill the promises. There are no reasons to doubt about the promises of Allāh, as these are always true.[10:4, 18:21, 18:98] In Sūrah An-Nahl, Allāh says:

Whoever does good, whether male or female,— provided he be a Believer, then We shall certainly cause him to live a happy life, and We shall invariably give them their reward in the best manner for what they used to do (An-Nahl 16:97).

In this verse, Allāh (swt) gives a clear promise under certain conditions. The promise is to give them a good life. The good life does not mean something that will happen in the Hereafter, but the good life will happen in this world. As in many promises that have conditions, Allāh also has some conditions before He will fulfill His promise. The conditions are: **(a)** we have to do good deeds, **(b)** it does not matter whether the person is a man or a woman and **(c)** that the person has to be a believer.

Human weakness to trust Allāh: Although we should not doubt the promises of Allāh, we tend to think He might not fulfill His promises. Many of us are weak in character, and we make and often break our promises. It is due to our weak character that we doubt about Allāh's promises. We may not admit, but our conduct often expresses that doubt. Here is an example. In verse 2:261 Allāh says:

مَّثَلُ ٱلَّذِينَ يُنفِقُونَ أَمْوَٰلَهُمْ فِى سَبِيلِ ٱللَّهِ كَمَثَلِ حَبَّةٍ أَنۢبَتَتْ سَبْعَ سَنَابِلَ فِى كُلِّ سُنۢبُلَةٍ مِّائَةُ حَبَّةٍ ۗ وَٱللَّهُ يُضَٰعِفُ لِمَن يَشَآءُ ۚ وَٱللَّهُ وَٰسِعٌ عَلِيمٌ ۝

The Parable of those who spend their wealth in the way of Allāh is like the parable of a grain which grows into seven ears, in every ear a hundred grains. And Allāh multiplies for whom He pleases; for Allāh is ample-Giving, all-Knowing.(Al Baqarah 2:261)

It is His promise that He will multiply our money if we spend on good causes. Yet when it comes to donating or spending money on a good cause, we often hesitate. We doubt whether we will ever get the return of the money. We think we might become a loser.

Allāh's promise with Mūsā (A): In the previous year we studied about prophet Mūsā. Let us recollect a part of his early life. There was a time when Fir'awn was torturing the Israelites in Egypt. He gave an order to kill all newborn Israelite male children and let the female children live.[2:49] When Mūsā was born, his mother was afraid for his life. She knew Fir'awn's people would kill her child. But Mūsā's mother was a believer and she was a righteous woman. She used to fulfill all three conditions we learned in verse 16:97 above. In verse 28:7 Allāh said:

And We revealed to the mother of Mūsā saying: "Nurse him; but when you fear for him, then cast him in the river, and do not fear and do not grieve. Surely We are going to give him back to you and make him a rasul."

Imagine the gravity of the situation. On one hand, Fir'awn was threatening to kill all male children. On the other hand, Allāh was telling her to cast the baby in the river. Both the situations seemed dangerous. However, Allāh made a promise here—He would unite the child with his mother. Not only that, He would make the child a prophet when he would grow up. So many promises! How can a common person trust such promises? Do we have strong *iman* to carry out such an order? Mūsā's mother had strong *iman*, and she responded to Allāh's promise. She knew casting infant Mūsā in the river might be very risky, but she was certain that Allāh's promises would never fail.

The incidents that followed were amazing. The basket in which infant Mūsā was placed continued to float in the river until it reached the palace of Fir'awn. The wife of Fir'awn picked up the basket and discovered the child. Even though she knew about Firʿawn's order to kill all male children of the Israelites, she did not worry. Even if she knew the baby was an Israelite, she made sure no one killed the child. She would adopt the child as her son.

Infant Mūsā, although safe now, was away from his mother. He continued to cry.[28:12] Mūsā's sister had secretly followed the basket and she knew where the basket reached. She came to the queen and told her about a woman who could nurse the baby. His sister did not disclose her identity or the identity of the woman who might feed him. Then she brought her own mother. Infant Mūsā liked her—and why not, she was after all his own mother. Thus, his mother was united with him and she was able to feed him.[28:13]

Thus Allāh quickly fulfilled His one promise. He returned Mūsā back to his mother. Not only that, now Mūsā began a new life in Firʿawn's palace as his adopted son—in a princely manner. He began receiving all good things in life. Eventually when he grew up Allāh made him a prophet. Thus Allāh fulfilled His other promise of making him a prophet.

Lesson for us: Mūsā's life shows us that no matter how critical and how difficult circumstances may be, Allāh's promise will always come true. We have to remember two things:

(a) we have to be a believer;

(b) we have to do good deeds.

If we fulfill these, Allāh will give us a good life here and in the Hereafter. We should remember

Allāh's promise is true and every promise will be fulfilled. We must trust Allāh and follow His commands. We pray to Him:

رَبَّنَا وَءَاتِنَا مَا وَعَدتَّنَا عَلَىٰ رُسُلِكَ وَلَا تُخْزِنَا يَوْمَ ٱلْقِيَٰمَةِ إِنَّكَ لَا تُخْلِفُ ٱلْمِيعَادَ ۝

Rabbanā wa ātinā mā waʿadtanā ʿalā rusulika wa lā tukhzinā yawma-l qiyāmat. Innaka lā tukhlifu-l mīʿād.

Our Rabb! and give us what You have promised us through Your rasuls, and do not disgrace us on the day of Awakening. Surely You do not break promise. (Al-i-ʿImran 3:194)

Our promises: Although we often make promises, we should remember that unless Allāh wills, we cannot do anything. Therefore, we must say *Insha-Allāh* (i.e. if Allāh wishes) after we promise anything.[18:23-24] We must not make meaningless promises, if we cannot keep them. The punishments for false promises are severe.[5:89]

homework**weekend 2**

1. What is a promise?

_____

_____

_____

2. How are promises of Allāh different from our promises?

_____

_____

3. Explain how Mūsā's mother responded to Allāh's command?

_____

_____

4. How did Allāh reunite Mūsā with his mother?

_____

_____

5. In order for Allāh's promises to become true, in sūrah An-Nahl, verse 97, Allāh said two things a person must do. What are the two things?

_____

_____

6. How many promises mentioned in the Qur'ān will be fulfilled? Select the correct choice.

    (a) About 50 promises will be fulfilled.
    (b) Some will be fulfilled some will not.
    (c) All promises will be fulfilled only in the Hereafter
    (d) All promises will be fulfilled in this world and in the Hereafter.

7. Memorize the duʿā mentioned in the lesson. In the next class, be ready to recite the duʿā.

Objective of the Qur'ān

Objective of the Lesson:

The Qur'ān has several different objectives. If we can understand these objectives, we can easily understand the message of the Qur'ān, follow its guidance and be good Muslims. This lesson discusses some of the objectives of the Qur'ān.

Imagine you parachuted in a tropical forest, deep and dark. You are alone, and you need to reach your base camp—which may be miles away in an unknown direction. What would you need to safely come out of the forest and reach the comfort of the base camp? I am sure, your list will include a survival guide, a map, a compass, and may be a flashlight if it gets dark. You wish someone had taught you how to find edible fruits, how to avoid poisonous plants, how to keep your energy and how to keep your cool.

Now let us look at another scene. We are in this world, and we have to reach our goal of becoming a good human being, a good Muslim. The world is full of traps and tricks. "Where is the map?" you ask. "What should I avoid and what should I collect? Where is the light that will show the path when life is pitch black with ignorance?"

The Qur'ān is the map: The Qur'ān is the map that shows us the Right Path. It tells us what to avoid and what to collect in our journey of this life. This manual is written by the Master Guide—Allāh (swt), who does not make any mistakes in guiding people.

The Qur'ān is the guidance: All of us want to be safe and successful, and Allāh (swt) wants

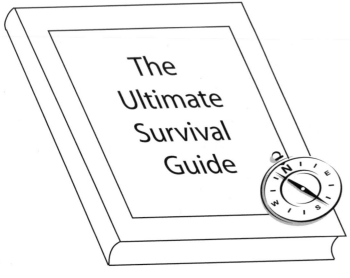

The Ultimate Survival Guide

the same for us. Therefore, Allāh (swt) has sent us the Qur'ān as a Guidance to lead our lives. This Guidance is similar to the map that was very useful in the tropical forest. Without that map you would have been wandering in the forest for days, and may have been attacked by a big cat. Similarly, without the Qur'ān we will be lost in our lives, and will be doing things which we should not be doing. The Qur'ān is the guidance for entire mankind.

The Qur'ān tells us how to find the Truth and how to avoid falsehood. It reminds us of the rewards that we can get if we follow its directions. The Qur'ān often gives us good news. It also warns us if we miss our tracks. It repeats some verses several times, because it is important that we understand the teaching very clearly.

What the Qur'ān is not: The Qur'ān is not a story book. It sometimes tells a parable, or a short story, to remind us what will happen if we do right or wrong. The Qur'ān often does not tell the details of a story, because it emphasizes on the teaching of the story without unnecessary details. The Qur'ān is not a history book either. It does not tell the history of prophets, but tells us what we can learn from the lives of the prophets.

How to live in a society: The Qur'ān wants us to live in a good society. Therefore, it tells us how to behave with other people, how to share with others and why not to hurt people. It tells us to stand up against bad things that may harm our society. It tells why we should be a team in a society. It does not want us to divide ourselves into small groups.

The Qur'ān gives us hope: The Qur'ān also gives us hope. The hope is

guaranteed by Allāh (swt). It tells us that even if we have a difficult life, we can ultimately be successful by remaining on the right track.

Eternal teachings: The teachings of the Qur'ān are valid forever. It has Guidance for people of all ages. When people followed the teachings of the Qur'ān, they became very successful. The Arab society was a lifeless system, but the Qur'ān gave a fresh life to it. A modern society can be equally successful by following Qur'ānic teachings.

One of the names of the Qur'ān is **al-Shifa** or the Healer. The Qur'ān heals the diseases in a person's mind; it heals the diseases that ruin a society.

The Qur'ān asks us to use our intelligence. It tells us to think about the teachings of the Qur'ān. If we can use our brain, we can progress in our lives. The Qur'ān asks us to deeply reflect about its message.

أَفَلَا يَتَدَبَّرُونَ ٱلْقُرْءَانَ أَمْ عَلَىٰ قُلُوبٍ أَقْفَالُهَآ ٢٤

What! will they not then ponder on the Qur'ān, or is it that on their hearts are locks? (47:24)

The Prophet (S) was the living example to prove that human beings can follow the instructions of the Qur'ān.

Since the Qur'ān is our Guide, we should always keep it handy. We should study it often. We will be successful if we follow its teachings. Allāh (swt) made the teachings simple and easy to remember.

Allāh (swt) wants us to lead a good life and have a good society. Therefore, He has blessed us with the finest Guidance and best Teachings in the Qur'ān.

homework**weekend 3**

1. Read Sūrah Az-Zumar, verse 27. Why did Allāh (swt) tell parables in the Qur'ān?

_____

2. Verse 9 of Sūrah Bani Isrā'īl or al-Isrā' tells two objectives of the Qur'ān. Write these objectives below:

     a. _____

     b. _____

3. Verse 29 of Sūrah Sād (Sūrah 38) tells two objectives of the Qur'ān. Write these objectives below:

     a. _____

     b. _____

4. Read the first two verses of Sūrah 55. Who is the best teacher of the Qur'ān?

_____

5. Verse 46:12 of Sūrah Al-Ahqāf tells two objectives of the Qur'ān. Write these objectives below: (Hint: the answer is in the second half of the verse)

     a. _____

     b. _____

6. To get the right guidance from the Qur'ān, what should we do before we recite it? Find the answer in Sūrah An-Nahl, verse 98.

_____

_____

_____

_____

Compilation of the Qur'ān

Objective of the Lesson:

The Qur'ān was revealed over a long twenty three years in bits and pieces. Its compilation was done in a very careful, systematic and orderly manner. This lesson discusses some of the ways the Qur'ān was compiled and preserved.

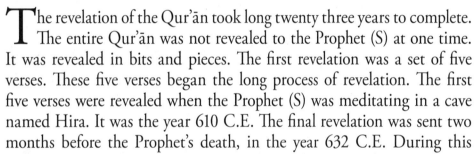

The revelation of the Qur'ān took long twenty three years to complete. The entire Qur'ān was not revealed to the Prophet (S) at one time. It was revealed in bits and pieces. The first revelation was a set of five verses. These five verses began the long process of revelation. The first five verses were revealed when the Prophet (S) was meditating in a cave named Hira. It was the year 610 C.E. The final revelation was sent two months before the Prophet's death, in the year 632 C.E. During this long period angel Jibril brought revelations to the Prophet (S). Sometimes he brought only one verse, sometimes a few verses and at other times an entire sūrah.

The question is: who compiled and recorded all these verses and sūrahs? How was the revelation arranged and compiled into one book? The Prophet (S) did not know how to read or write. Therefore, the other question is: who wrote down the revelation after it reached the Prophet (S)? All these are good questions. In this lesson we will try to find the answers.

Compilation at the time of the Prophet (S): The Prophet (S) adopted three methods to compile the revelation. When a revelation reached him, first he immediately memorized it. After he recited the revelation, in the second step one of his companions immediately wrote down the revelation. In the third step the companions memorized the revelation. For a long twenty three years, the entire Qur'ān was recorded, compiled and preserved in this manner. As more and more people accepted Islam, the number of people who memorized the Qur'ān increased.

Written record: Memorization of the Qur'ān was not enough to preserve it. Imagine, what would happen when people who memorized it died? If there was no written document, the revelation would be lost. Therefore, the Qur'ān had to be recorded on paper. But the Prophet (S) did not know how to write. It was not a problem. We have already mentioned that many of the companions knew how to write. They wrote it down and read it out to the Prophet (S) to verify if the writing was correct and accurate. One of the famous companions who wrote down the Qur'ān was **Zaid ibn Thabit**. When Zaid was not present, other companions wrote down the revelation. As many as forty different companions wrote down at least one or more of the verses under direct supervision of the Prophet (S). Writing down was so important that wherever the Prophet (S) went, people used to carry pens, inkstands and writing materials with them. They wrote it down on papers, parchments, dry skins of animals, dry leaves and on other materials.

Compilation by the Prophet (S): The order in which we find the Qur'ān today was not the order in which it was revealed. For example: sūrah Fātihah is the first chapter in the Qur'ān but it was not the first revelation. The first revelation was five verses that got compiled into sūrah number 96. The name of the sūrah is **al-'Alaq**. Different parts of the Qur'ān were revealed at different times. Whenever the Prophet (S) received a revelation, he told his companions under which chapter the revelation should be recorded. In this process the Qur'ān was recorded under direct supervision of the Prophet (S). By the time twenty three years passed and the revelation got completed, the Prophet (S) made sure the correct verse was recorded under the correct chapter.

Compilation after the Prophet (S): Although the Prophet (S) arranged all the verses in the Qur'ān, it was not made into a book. After the Prophet (S) passed away, Abū Bakr was appointed as the Khalīfa of the Muslim community. Abū Bakr realized he should collect all the chapters of the Qur'ān and bring them under one volume. The whole Qur'ān was already written down as manuscripts, but the manuscripts were scattered and stored with different companions. Under Abū Bakr's supervision, the scattered chapters of the Qur'ān were compiled. Accuracy of the manuscripts was verified with many of the companions who memorized the Qur'ān. Then it was compiled in

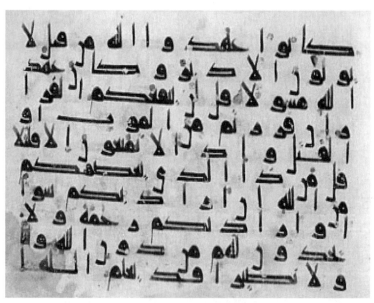

the same sequence as the Prophet (S) had wanted and suggested. Even then a complete book was not produced. When Abū Bakr died, the compiled volume was transferred to the custody of 'Umar, the second Khalīfa. When Khalīfa 'Umar died, the volume was transferred to the custody of 'Umar's daughter Hafsa. She was one of the wives of the Prophet (S).

Role Of 'Uthmān Ibn Affan: When 'Uthman became the Khalīfa, the territories of the Muslim world already expanded. Parts of Iraq and Africa were under Muslim rule. The population of the Muslims also increased. It was no more possible to memorize the Qur'ān from recitation of another person. A book was needed. 'Uthman feared that unless the Qur'ān was compiled into one single book, people might add a verse in it or forget a verse.

'Uthman collected the official copy of the Qur'ān that Abū Bakr had collected and made several copies of the original version. There was no printing press at that time. Therefore the extra copies had to be copied by hand. Then he ordered all other personal copies of the Qur'ān should be destroyed. He circulated the official copy to people everywhere. He ordered people should memorize the Qur'ān from the official copies only. 'Uthman sent the official copies to all the governors in Muslim occupied territories. All the later day Muslims learned, memorized and made additional copies of the Qur'ān from these official copies circulated by 'Uthman.

Allāh preserves the Qur'ān: The Prophet (S) and his companions made sure every word of the original revelation got compiled into the Qur'ān. These are all human efforts. Sometimes human efforts may fail. For this reason, Allāh says in the Qur'ān He is the actual guardian of the Qur'ān.

$$إِنَّا نَحْنُ نَزَّلْنَا ٱلذِّكْرَ وَإِنَّا لَهُۥ لَحَٰفِظُونَ ۝$$

Surely We ourselves revealed the reminder and We most certainly are its Guardian (15:9).

Since Allāh is the guardian of the Qur'ān, He preserved the reliability of the text from all type of human error or natural destruction. He made sure no new words were introduced in the Qur'ān and no original revelation was deleted from the compilation. The Qur'ān we read today is the same Qur'ān revealed to the Prophet (S) more than fourteen hundred years ago.

Interesting Facts:

The Arabic calligraphy was developed due to the tremendous respect provided in writing the Qur'ān.

Popular calligraphic styles include kufi and naksh. Kufi writing is angular in nature, while naksh is cursive.

The Arabic alphabets were employed to write other languages, such as Persian and Urdu.

The early copies of the Qur'ān were without the vowel marks. The vowel marks were added later, so that the non-Arabs could properly pronounce the words.

1. Circle the letter **T** if the statement is correct, circle the letter **F** if it is false.

Zaid Ibn Thabit was one of the famous companions who wrote down the Qur'ān.   T   F

The companions arranged the verses, since the Prophet (S) did not know writing.   T   F

'Uthman burned all official copies of the Qur'ān and circulated the personal copies.   T   F

Arrangement of the Qur'ānic verses does not reflect the order they were revealed.   T   F

The longest sūrahs were revealed first, the shortest sūrahs were revealed later.   T   F

2. Mention three ways the Prophet (S) made sure all revelations were written down and preserved.

(a) _____

(b) _____

(c) _____

3. Do you think any verses of the Qur'ān were dropped or deleted during compilation? Explain your answer.

_____

_____

_____

4. Mention two most significant things 'Uthmān did to preserve the accuracy and authenticity of the Qur'ān.

(a) _____

(b) _____

5. The accuracy of preservation and compilation is also indirectly mentioned in verse 4:82. Read the verse and mention what we cannot find in the Qur'ān?

_____

Previous Scriptures and the Qur'ān

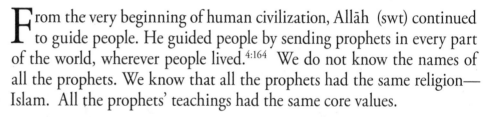

Objective of the Lesson:

The Qur'ān recognizes the previous scriptures sent by Allāh. Some of the scriptures are mentioned by name in the Qur'ān. What happened to these previous scriptures? What is the relation between the Qur'ān and these scriptures? This lesson discusses some of the scriptures and their relation with the Qur'ān.

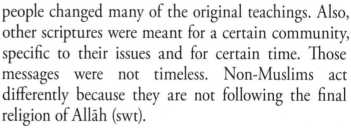

From the very beginning of human civilization, Allāh (swt) continued to guide people. He guided people by sending prophets in every part of the world, wherever people lived.[4:164] We do not know the names of all the prophets. We know that all the prophets had the same religion—Islam. All the prophets' teachings had the same core values.

Similar and dissimilar messages: Since all the prophets taught the same fundamental message, you will find many similar messages in other religions. You will find people of other religions have the same values—they discourage stealing, killing, or hurting others. However, their every action is not the same as the actions of a true Muslim. This is because people changed many of the original teachings. Also, other scriptures were meant for a certain community, specific to their issues and for certain time. Those messages were not timeless. Non-Muslims act differently because they are not following the final religion of Allāh (swt).

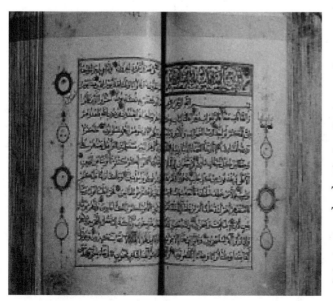

What happened to previous scriptures: Islam teaches us to believe in all prophets, and their scriptures. Unfortunately, we do not have those original scriptures. They have been destroyed or changed to some extent. The Jews today read their scripture called the Torah or the Tawrāt. The Christians read the Bible. Although these are the books revealed by Allāh, according to Islam, the present teachings in these books are not the same message originally revealed. People deleted some of the messages and added new messages that appeared suitable to them. They edited the content of the original messages.

The Qur'ān is the Guardian: One of the names of the Qur'ān is **al-Muhaimin** or the Guardian of previous scriptures. This means that the Qur'ān guards the true messages from the previous scriptures. Despite all the changes in the previous scriptures, they still contain many good teachings. They still contain the message to worship none but one God.

Role of the previous scriptures: Since the previous scriptures were meant for specific societies and specific times, some of the religious rules differ from one scripture to another. 'Isā (A) had modified some of the rules in the Torah. Similarly,

the Qur'ān also modified some rules of the Torah and the Injīl. The Qur'ān did not change any of its own rules.

Stories and explanations: The Qur'ān has many narratives of the past prophets that are also mentioned in the Tawrāt and the Injīl. The Qur'ānic narratives are not in detail. Since the Qur'ān does not tell stories, we should not use other scriptures to explain an incident mentioned in the Qur'ān. The incidents mentioned in other scriptures may have been modified; therefore we trust the description as we find in the Qur'ān. Since the Qur'ān is called **al-Furqan** or the Discriminator, it distinguishes the facts from the fiction in other scriptures.

The messages in other scriptures were partial. The Qur'ān brings the complete message as it states:

$$ٱلْيَوْمَ أَكْمَلْتُ لَكُمْ دِينَكُمْ وَأَتْمَمْتُ عَلَيْكُمْ نِعْمَتِى وَرَضِيتُ لَكُمُ ٱلْإِسْلَٰمَ دِينًا$$

*"…This day I have **perfected** for you your religion, and **completed** upon you My blessings, and have accepted for you Islam as the religion…"* (Sūrah Al-Mā'idah 5:3).

Protection of the past scriptures: Allāh did not want to protect the messages of previous scriptures. There is no need to protect those scriptures, as they were meant for small societies and for short period of human civilization. Allāh protects the messages of the Qur'ān as a "Tablet well guarded" or **lauhe mahfuz**.[85:21-22] In another ayah, Allāh says that He is the protector of the Qur'ān.[15:9]

$$إِنَّا نَحْنُ نَزَّلْنَا ٱلذِّكْرَ وَإِنَّا لَهُ لَحَٰفِظُونَ ۝$$

Surely We Ourselves revealed the Reminder, and We most certainly are its Guardian. (15:9)

There are many ways the Qur'ān is being protected in this world. People still read the Qur'ān in the same Arabic words that were revealed to Prophet Muhammad (S). People of other religion usually do not read their scriptures in the original language. They read from a translation only. Muslims memorize the original Arabic Qur'ān. They also record the Qur'ān in all kinds of available writing media— paper, leather, and computer disks. Many mosques have the whole Qur'ān curved out in stone on their walls.

When people of other

divine religions call Allāh (swt) as God, Eloheim or Ishwar, they are not calling a different deity. They are calling Allāh (swt) in their own languages. Allāh (swt) had sent scriptures to other communities in their own languages so that they could understand.

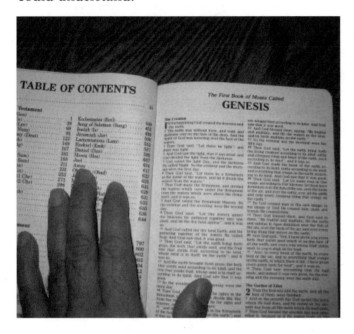

Can we read other scriptures: When we grow up we may study other scriptures. Studying other scriptures could enhance your knowledge. However, before we study other scriptures, we should first make sure we study the Qur'ān thoroughly. Many of the things mentioned in the previous scriptures are different from the message of the Qur'ān. We should remember the Qur'ān is our ultimate guide and we should take all guidance and directions from the Qur'ān.

Respect other scriptures: We should always respect good things around us. When it comes to the previous scriptures, we should certainly respect them. These scriptures do contain remains of original divine teachings. Even though there is little benefit for us from the previous scriptures, we should never disrespect them. We should remember and understand that as we do not like anyone to disrespect the Qur'ān, we should not disrespect the previous scriptures.

homework**weekend 5**

1. Why was the Qur'ān sent to Muhammad (S) in Arabic? (Find the answer in Sūrah Az-Zukhruf, verse 3).

_____

2. Sūrah Al-Qasas, verse 49 says: "*You say: Bring then a scripture from the presence of Allāh, which is a better guide than these two,—I shall follow it,—if you are truthful*". Of the two Books, one is the Qur'ān, which is the other one? (Find the hint for your answer in the previous verse, i.e., Al-Qasas, verse 48).

_____

3. Read Sūrah Al-Hijr, verse 9. Who is the Guardian of the Qur'ān?

_____

4. Read the complete translation of the following two verses and then fill up the statement given below:

"Indeed We have revealed the Tawrāt—in it there is guidance and light...." (5:44)

"...and We gave him ('Isā) the Injīl in which there is guidance and light...." (5:46)

What are common between Tawrāt and Injīl? _____

_____.

5. Read verse 37 of Sūrah Yūnus. Then circle **T** if the sentence is correct and circle **F** if it is incorrect.

a. Parts of the Qur'ān may have been written by scholars.	T	F
b. The Qur'ān confirms scriptures before it.	T	F
c. The Qur'ān does not explain other Books or itself.	T	F
d. There are doubtful parables in the Qur'ān.	T	F

Importance of Shahādah

Objective of the Lesson:

Shahādah is not just a sentence we declare to become Muslim. The importance of Shahādah is much more than a mere sentence. We have to live by the spirit of Shahādah. This lesson emphasizes the importance and shows the students how they can live by the spirit of Shahādah.

In Islam, Shahādah means declaration of the faith. It is a verbal form of giving testimony or witness. We can give witness when we know something clearly. In the religion of Islam **La ilaha illa-l lah, Muhammadur rasulullah** is called the Shahādah.

When we translate, it means

La ilaha illa-l lah: There is no deity but Allāh.

Muhammadur rasulullah: Muhammad is the Messenger of Allāh.

The complete Shahādah: It is a practice to state the complete Shahādah in Arabic. Complete Shahādah is an expanded form of the Shahādah. It is as follows:

Ash-hadu anla ilaha illal-Lahu Wahdahu la Sharika Lahu wa-ash-hadu anna Muhammadan abduhu wa rasuluhu.

The English translation: The English translation of the complete Shahādah is as follows:

I bear witness that there is none worthy of worship except Allāh, the One, without any partner. And I bear witness that Muhammad is His servant and His Messenger.

When we state the Shahādah, in full knowledge of its meaning, we become Muslims. Without the declaration of Shahādah we are not Muslims. Therefore declaration of Shahādah is called the first pillar of Islam.

The scope of Shahādah: The scope of Shahādah is much more than loudly reciting it. It is a part of our life. We live by this statement and we work by the principle of this statement.

The first part: The first part of the statement means there is no one worthy of worshipping other than Allāh (swt). In the first part of Shahādah see how the statement is presented. The sentence starts with *La ilaha*. The word "la" means "no." The word "ilaha" means god or anything that people may worship, i.e. a deity. In the Shahādah first we declare there is no possibility of any god or godly things or deities to exist. Once we eliminate all possibilities of other gods or deities to exist, then we declare *illa-l-llah*. This means except Allāh. Allāh (swt) is our only Master. He created us and sustains us. We are always in need of Allāh (swt). Without the help of Allāh (swt), we cannot do anything. We worship only Allāh (swt).

The second part: The second part of the statement confirms that we do not worship Muhammad (S). He was a rasul, which means he brought messages from Allāh (swt). We believe the messages in the Qur'an. Muhammad (S) did not leave behind a family to rule over the Muslims. He did not even leave a picture of himself for the future generations. Muhammad (S) was not a deity; he was not a son of Allāh (swt). Since he was the prophet of Allāh (swt), we follow his teachings and the Book that he received.

False deities: Worshipping a deity does not always mean that somebody has to go to a temple to worship an idol. People worship idols at home, at work, everywhere. Sometimes deities are idols made by men, sometimes some people claim they are the deities. You will find many people worship other human beings.

All human being who claim they are god are liars. They are the scam artist. They fool people and trick them to buy expensive gifts for the false gods.

All men who claim to be god or divine are fraud. They use other people's weakness to rob them of their money and freedom. They give false hope to people, but cannot actually give anything.

Most of their promises are tricks—they will say "You will get good grades in your exam only if you donate money to my temple with an open mind". Now, if you fail even after donating the money, he will say "your mind was not open, you have to donate more." Anyway, he made his money and you lost yours.

Other form of deity: Not all such frauds will claim they are god or divine. Some of them will become the ruler of a country by force. They ask people to follow them without any question. They make people slaves under their rule. People work for them as labors without any benefit. In the past Pharaoh treated his people as slaves. He oppressed them and killed the male child of the Israelites. He told them he was their god. There were and still are many such people who oppress others. Some of them may not even be the ruler of a country.

We do not want to be a slave under another person. At the same time, we do not want to be a dictator over another or community. A dictator

is someone who rules people by force, without mercy and without giving any benefit to the people. The dictators are bully. We do not want to be a bully, or be ruled by a bully. Some are political dictators, some are religious dictators. Some religious dictators will say you cannot reach Allāh (swt) without going through them. They make people believe that they are the gatekeepers. They are liars. Then they ask for money to open the gate.

There are some who are intellectual dictators. This type of dictators will not allow you to use your mind. They will not allow you to grow to your full extent. They want you to remain dull, so that they can control you. If you become smarter than them, then they cannot rule you. This is why they try to put a limit on your thinking.

By stating the Shahādah and following it in action, we become free from the evil clutches of those people who rule us physically, religiously, financially and intellectually. No human or other creature has any power to give life. None is eternal. The false deities, whether man or idols set up by man, have only one aim—they want to benefit at our cost.

We have only one Master, who is not interested in our wealth or service. He is One and Only Allāh (swt). Allāh (swt) does not want any money from us. He does not want us to work hard for His benefit. He wants us to open up our mind, think and be intelligent. He wants us to be happy and successful. He wants us to work for ourselves and our society.

from hadith

It is narrated on the authority of Abu Ayyub that a man came to the Prophet (S) and said: Direct me to a deed which draws me near to Paradise and takes me away from the Fire of Hell. Upon this the Prophet (S) said: You worship Allāh and never associate anything with Him, establish prayer, and pay zakāt, and do good to your kin. When he turned his back, the Prophet (S) said: If he adheres to what he has been ordered to do, he would enter Paradise. (Muslim).

1. Allāh (swt) is One and Only, and nobody can be equal to Him. This statement is stated in a Sūrah, whose translation is as follows: SAY: "*He is Allāh, the One, Allāh, the eternal Refuge. He does not beget, nor is He begotten; and no one can become equal to Him.*"

    a. Which Sūrah is this? _____ (Hint: This Sūrah is towards the end of the Qur'ān).

    b. What does it mean by "He does not beget, nor is He begotten"?

_____

_____

2. Sūrah An-Nāzi'āt, verse 79:24 mentions a man who had claimed "I am your lord, the most high". Who was this person? (Hint: you have to trace back seven verses to find his name).

_____

3. Read Sūrah Al-Hajj, verse 73. Then answer the following:

    a. What kind of insect is mentioned? _____

    b. Who cannot create this insect? _____

    c. Why is the insect more powerful? _____

_____

4. Read Sūrah Al-A'rāf, verse 3. Then answer the following:

    a. What should we NOT do? _____

_____

Compilation of Hadīth

Objective of the Lesson:

The process of compilation of Hadīth was very methodical and scientific. This lesson discusses some of the collectors and how they collected and compiled the Hadīth. This lesson is intended to help the students to respect and follow ahadīth in their true spirit.

The **Sunnah** and the **Hadīth** are critical parts of Islam. The word "sunnah" indicates the way of the life of the Prophet (S). The term Hadīth is narration about the life of the Prophet (S). It also includes things he said or things he did. Plural of Hadīth is **Ahādīth**.

In the beginning, all ahādīth were remembered and transmitted orally. For nearly one hundred years, people continued to passed down ahādīth orally from one person to another person. At a much later time Hadīth was recorded in a written form. In this lesson, we will study about compilation and collection of the Hadīth. We will also briefly study about the famous collectors of the Hadīth.

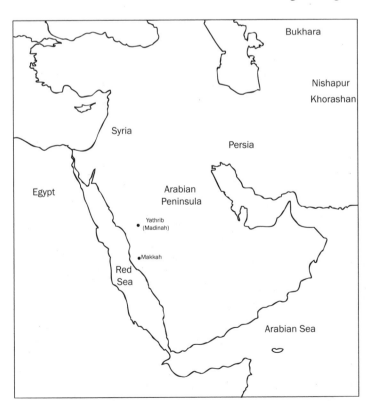

Compilation of Hadīth: The narration of ahādīth took place over a long period of time. During that time, some of the close companions of the Prophet (S) or the immediate followers of the companions were alive. The companions narrated various ahādīth that were eventually collected into books.

When the Prophet (S) was alive, there were very little written records of Hadīth. Many of the companions, or Sahābah, (sing. Sahābi) memorized the sayings of the Prophet (S). If there was any disagreement about any Hadīth, the Sahābah directly verified with the Prophet (S). Everything that the Prophet (S) said was fresh in people's memory. During this period Hadīth was mostly transmitted orally.

After the Prophet (S) passed away, the Sahābah continued to transmit Hadīth orally. Some of the companions began to write down the ahadīth. Most of these writings were for personal use. In about sixty or seventy years after the Prophet (S) passed away, most of his companions were no more alive.

Many Sahābah had their own follower and descendants. These followers are called **Tābi'in**. They realized that unless the ahadīth were written down, people might forget or mix up the sayings of the Prophet (S). Also, during their time the Islamic empire spread in the entire Middle East and beyond. It was not possible for people residing in far off places to hear the ahadīth from someone's mouth. They needed written records. They also needed to determine the genuine Hadīth from a large number of false ones that people began to invent. As a result, many famous Tābi'in began collecting Hadīth. **Imam Abu Hanifa, Imam Malik, Imam Shāfi'i** and **Imam Hanbal** were the most famous Tābi'in who collected large number of Hadīth.

After the Tābi'in passed away, their follower and descendants continued to collect Hadīth. These followers are called **Taba Tābi'in**.

How the collection was done: The collectors of Hadīth spent hours, days, months and years to collect genuine Hadīth and eliminate bad or forged ones. They checked the sources of Hadīth. If a person quoted a Hadīth, the collectors verified the sources from where the person heard the Hadīth. Most likely he heard it from his father or someone in the family or from another elderly person. That person must have heard it from another ancestor. This way the chain or sources were investigated until the original source was close to the Prophet (S). The long chain of narrators is called **isnad**. If the chain or narrators could not be determined, the particular Hadīth could not be verified as true.

Six major books of Hadīth: Based on the works of the Tābi'in, six Imams collected and compiled Hadīth. Their works are the most authentic. Over a period of time these six collections earned the name **Sahih Sittah** or Six Correct Books. They became the standard works of Hadīth collection. These six collections eventually became known by the name of the collectors. They are as follows:

1. Bukhārī
2. Muslim
3. Ibn Mājāh
4. Abu Dawūd
5. Tirmidhī
6. Nasā'ī

Imam Bukhārī: He was born in Bukhara in present day Uzbekistan. During childhood he was blind but later he regained his vision. He had remarkable memory and could narrate thousands of Hadīth accurately. During his lifetime he memorized more than 300,000 Hadīth. He was highly respected for his extraordinary intellect. He traveled to Nishapur, Samarkand and Baghdad. Wherever he went, people liked him, but in each place some people became envious of him and banished him.

Imam Muslim: Imam Muslim was born in Nishapur in Persia. He traveled extensively in Arabia, Egypt, Syria and Iraq to collect Hadīth. He had many students who collected Hadīth.

Ibn Mājāh: He collected about 4,000 Hadīth and compiled them in 32 volumes. Today his work is not equally valued as the works of Bukhārī or Muslim. Some of his collections appear to be weak.

Abu Dawūd: He was a famous collector of Hadīth. He was born in Sijistan in Iran. Like all other Hadīth collectors, he too traveled widely. He was mainly interested in law, and as a result his collection mainly focuses on legal ahādīth. He collected about 50,000 ahādīth from which he chose 4,800 for compilation.

Tirmidhī: He was a student of Imam Muslim and Abu Dawūd. Not much details can be found about his life. He lived in Khorasan, Iraq, and Hejaz. Most of the Hadīth that he collected are related to law and rules and regulations.

Nasā'ī: He was a famous collector of Hadīth. He was born in Nasā (in Khorasan) and traveled extensively to collect Hadīth. He lived in Egypt for a while, and then in Damascus. He died in 915 C.E. His collection is known as Sunan al-Sughra or as Sunan an-Nasā'ī.

Note: C.E. stands for Common Era. The numbering of the year is identical to A.D. system. Common Era is preferred since it does not have any religious titles referring to Jesus Christ.

1. What is the meaning of Sahih Sitta?

_____

2. What was the need for collecting ahādīth?

_____

_____

_____

3. Imam Bukhārī had retained about 7,000 ahādīth as reliable out of about 600,000 that he collected. About how many were considered not reliable?

_____

_____

4. Imam Bukhārī was born in a city called Bukhara (also spelt Bokhara). Can you find out where Bukhara is located? Use your atlas or the Internet to find this town and write down the findings.

_____

5. Which of the following choices is correct about Hadīth collection and transmission AT THE TIME of the Prophet (S)?

    (a)   Most of the Hadīth were collected in a single volume.
    (b)   All the companions wrote down a large number of Hadīth.
    (c)   Most of the Hadīth were orally transmitted.
    (d)   People began writing down Sahih Sittah.

6. The following may be the reasons why people began collecting Hadīth. Circle **T** if the statement is True, circle **F** if the statement is false.

    (a)   Fear that very soon people might forget the sayings of the Prophet (S).   T   F
    (b)   Written form of Hadīth was needed for people living in far off places.   T   F
    (c)   Eliminate the bad Hadīth and keep only the genuine ones.   T   F
    (d)   Hadīth was needed for the people who cannot speak Arabic.   T   F

Nūh (A): *Truth is Most Important*

Objective of the Lesson:

The history of prophet Nūh (A) is dramatic and informative. History shows that Allāh always helps the righteous people and those who obey Him. History also shows that Allāh does not save the wrongdoers even if they think they can save themselves. It is not just a story, but we have lessons to learn so that we can seek Allāh's protection and blessings.

The incidents about prophet Nūh (A) are mentioned in many different sūrah in the Qur'ān. Nūh was the most important prophet to come after prophet Ādam but before prophet Ibrāhīm. The Christians and the Jews respect him as a great prophet. His biblical name is Noah. The stories of Nūh in the Bible and the Torah are somewhat different from what the Qur'ān tells us. If we study all the Qur'ānic verses related to Nūh, we can get a clear picture about his mission and teachings.

Like all other prophets, Nūh also faced a very bad community. His community was destroyed after they refused to be guided.

Teachings of Nūh: Prophet Nūh came to a community that was living an immoral life. They used to worship idols. They had many different idols, each had different names. Prophet Nūh told them the core message of Islam—to worship one God. He told his people: *O my people, serve Allāh; you have no deity other than Him. Surely I fear for you the punishment of a Mighty Day.*[7:59]

Only a few people believed him. The leaders among the rest of the people laughed at Nūh. They refused to believe in Nūh's message. They thought Nūh could not be a prophet since he was only a human being.

The leaders told their people, *"He is nothing but a man like yourselves, he wants to assert superiority over you. And had Allāh wanted, He could surely have sent down angels: we have not heard this among our fathers of the past."*[23:24]

Most of the people listened to the leaders. They refused to accept Nūh's teaching and guidance.

Nūh's miserable life: People made Nūh's life miserable by taunting him and laughing at him. The leaders were more nasty with him. They challenged Nūh to bring upon them any punishment if he were a truthful person.[11:32] Nūh knew he did not have any power to destroy anyone. He knew such power is only with Allāh. Nūh continued to appeal to his people to believe in Allāh and the people continued to ignore him.

Nūh did not loose hope. He depended upon Allāh and prayed to Him for support. The people started to call him a liar,[11:27] a man possessed by devil.[23:25] Saddened by such taunting, Nūh prayed to Allāh saying:

$$ رَبِّ ٱنصُرۡنِي بِمَا كَذَّبُونِ ۝ $$

My Rabb! help me because they belie me.(23:26)

Lesson from Allāh's help: Allāh told Nūh to build a boat on dry land.[11:37] Now think of it. Already people were laughing at him for teaching about one God. Now he was going to build a big boat on a dry land! It must have been very difficult for him to understand Allāh's plan. But he did not question. He followed Allāh's command and started building a boat with wooden plank tied with palm coir.[54:13] Every time people passed by, they laughed at him. To annoy him they asked why he was building a boat on dry land. It was the biggest joke of the town! The people were convinced that Nūh was a crazy person or some devils possessed him. But Nūh remained committed to Allāh. Even if it did not make sense to anybody, he continued to build the boat.

The Qur'ān wants us to learn a lesson from the dedication of Nūh. As long as he knew he was in the right path, nothing mattered to him.

The purpose of building the boat: After the construction of the boat was over, one day it started to rain. The rain continued for days. All the ponds, lakes, rivers got filled with water. The water started to spill over the land. Soon everything on the ground was under water. Nūh boarded the boat along with a small number of people who believed him. He also boarded a pair of all domestic animals on the boat. As the waves became stronger, the boat started to rock. Nūh was not a professional boat-builder. It seemed like the boat would sink! Nūh had complete faith upon Allāh. He knew as long as he was on the right path and sought help from Allāh, he would be safe. So he sincerely prayed:

$$ بِسۡمِ ٱللَّهِ مَجۡر۪ىٰهَا وَمُرۡسَىٰهَآ إِنَّ رَبِّي لَغَفُورٌ رَّحِيمٌ ۝ $$

With the name of Allāh be its sailing and its anchoring. Surely my Rabb is indeed Protector, most Rewarding. (11:41)

Truth is most important: Nūh's wife was a disbeliever. Nūh had a son who was also a disbeliever. When flood came, Nūh thought he should pick up his son on the boat. When he called his son to join him on the boat, he refused.[11:43] The evil son thought he did not require help from his father or from Allāh. He thought he would climb a mountain and be saved, but the water level continued to rise. The son was not saved, he was drowned in the flood. Nūh had to give up his own family members for the sake of truth. Allāh told him that such evil son did not deserve to be in his family. Then Nūh apologized to Allāh for his initial desire to save his son.[11:44]

Lessons we can apply today: In our daily life we may come across many temptations to move away from the right path. Our mind may tell us to give up the right path just because someone else would be laughing at us. For example, many of us skip Dhuhr or 'Asr salāt at school or workplace since we fear what others would say or what if others laugh at us. Nūh's example teaches us as long we are in the right path, we should not worry about what others say.

Nūh's son felt he was self-sufficient, he had no need of Allāh's help. He thought if he climbed the mountain he would be saved. Unless Allāh helps, nobody or nothing can help us.

We will often face difficult times in our lives. We should never give up hope and always seek help from Allāh. Only if Allāh is our protector and helper, we can hope to be safe and secure in life.

A new beginning: After a few days the flood water receded. The evil community was destroyed in the flood water. Nūh and his followers landed safely from the boat. They had their animals and belongings to start a new life again.

Interesting Facts:

Nūh (A) had used *dusur*, a rope made from oakum or palm fibers, to build his boat. Just as with other correct information in the Qur'an, modern scientists are agreeing to this fact as valid for early ship building techniques.

The *dusur* can also be tree nails. These were used in olden days to join wooden planks.

Nūh had used the best boat building technology available at that time. Much later, in 2,500 B.C.E., Khufu, the Pharaoh, had also built a ship with wooden planks.

The oldest boats discovered by the archeologists are the ones in Abydos, Egypt. These boats, built about 5,000 years back, were also made with wooden planks connected together by ropes.

Nūh could not have used iron nails for his boat. Iron was discovered much later, at the time of Dāwūd (A), who used iron swords and iron mails as armors.

homework**weekend 8**

1. In the Qur'ān there is a sūrah named after Nūh. What is the number of the sūrah and where was it revealed?

_____

2. Righteous people are often insulted by bad people. Nūh was insulted by his people. Write below two insulting names the people used against Nūh.

    (a)   In 23:25 _____

    (b)   In 54:9 _____

3. Read verse 11:45. Why did Nūh want to save his son?

_____

4. Read verse 11:46. What was the reason Nūh's son would not be saved?

_____

5. When Nūh was teaching Allāh's message to his people, who opposed him the most?

    (a)   The women.
    (b)   The leaders.
    (c)   The children.
    (d)   The angels.

6. People of Nūh refused to believe in him because he was a human being. They thought God should send His message through someone else. Who did they mean should have been sent by God?

    (a)   Adam.
    (b)   Women.
    (c)   Angel.
    (d)   Muhammad (S).

7. Find the words: NUH, ALLAH, FLOOD, BOAT, ANIMAL, PAIR, MOUNTAIN, LAUGH

A	M	O	U	N	T	A	I	N
K	F	C	A	G	B	R	A	D
P	W	F	L	O	O	D	N	E
A	X	T	L	S	A	A	I	N
I	W	H	A	O	T	E	M	P
R	N	U	H	L	M	J	A	T
P	A	L	A	U	G	H	L	B

Tālūt, Jālūt and Dāwūd(A)

Objective of the Lesson:

The history of these three people carries great moral lesson for all of us. Who were Tālūt and Jālūt and how were they involved in the history of prophet Dāwūd (A)? The lesson aims to describe the fascinating details about these three people, and the struggle of Dāwūd (A) in the path of Allāh.

The Qur'ān has a beautiful story about the rise of Dāwūd (A) as a king of the Israelites. This is a story of patience and perseverance of a few rightly guided people. The story tells us Allāh helps those who follow the right path and remain committed to establish law and order.

We are going to study about the rise of Dāwūd as the king. In the story there are two other characters. They are Tālūt and Jālūt.

The early beginning: A long time back, Mūsā (A) rescued the Israelites from Egypt and made them an independent nation. The Israelites settled in Canaan in ancient Palestine. Living in Canaan for hundreds of years was not peaceful for the Israelites. They were constantly suffering threats at the hand of other tribes. They realized they needed a king. A new king who would guide them to fight in the path of Allāh.[2:246] In response to the wish of the Israelites, their prophet announced that the king would be Tālūt.[2:247] His biblical name is Saul. The prophet is mentioned in the Bible as Samuel.

War breaks out: After Tālūt became the king, a war broke out between the Israelites and the Philistines. The Philistines were a ferocious tribe. Their leader was Jālūt—a very well built and skillful warrior. In the Bible Jālūt is mentioned as **Goliath**. The people

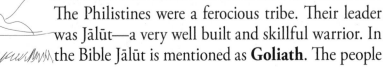

were scared of him for his bravery and ferocity. They believed nobody could defeat the Philistine army as long as Jālūt was their warrior.

Prayer for Victory: When war broke out, Tālūt marched with his army to face Jālūt and his ferocious army. Tālūt's army was small. His army included Dāwūd and his brothers. During the march to the battle, Tālūt and Dāwūd prayed to Allāh with a beautiful du'ā:

رَبَّنَآ أَفۡرِغۡ عَلَيۡنَا صَبۡرًا وَثَبِّتۡ أَقۡدَامَنَا وَٱنصُرۡنَا عَلَى ٱلۡقَوۡمِ ٱلۡكَـٰفِرِينَ ۞

Rabbana afrig 'alaynā sabraw wa thabbit aqdāmanā wa ansurnā 'alal qawmil kāfirīn.

Our Rabb! Pour down upon us perseverance and make our feet firm and help us against the unbelieving people (2:250).

In this prayer Tālūt and Dāwūd prayed for three things for their army:

(a) perseverance

(b) firm feet and

(c) help

Perseverance was needed because the battle was tough and it required all out effort from the army. They needed strong willpower and dedication to fight without fear. They knew Allāh can give them the power and courage to persevere.

Firm feet was needed because someone might behave cowardly. They could not afford to turn back and leave the battle. They have to fight until the battle was won.

Help from Allāh was needed because without Allāh's help nothing can be successful.

Confrontation with Jālūt: Finally in the battlefield the Israelites came face to face with Jālūt and his mighty army. Everybody was terrified at the sight of the monstrous Goliath. The custom of that time

was before battle starts, two warriors fight a duel. During the time of the Prophet (S), in the battle of Badr and Uhud the Muslims and Quraish fought duels before the actual battle.

Jālūt came forward to fight the duel. Everybody in Tālūt's army was terrified. They knew fighting a duel with Jālūt meant death. Nobody was coming forward to fight the duel. It was a disgrace for Tālūt. He offered the hand of his daughter in marriage to the man who would fight Jālūt. Even then nobody came forward. Ultimately young Dāwūd came forward to fight the duel.

Dāwūd and Jālūt: The moment Dāwūd came forward, everybody from the enemy's side roared into a laughter. Goliath taunted young Dāwūd and refused to fight him because he was no match for him. He wanted a true warrior to show off his skills. But Dāwūd challenged Goliath with the name of

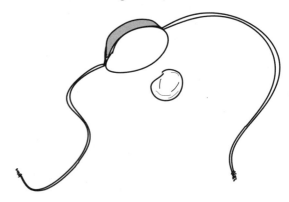

Allāh. He was not scared of him because he knew Allāh would help him. He taunted Goliath saying his armor, sword or battle skill would not help him today. Goliath's pride was hurt. Finally he agreed to fight the young boy.

Young Dāwūd did not know fighting very well. He knew he could not beat Goliath in a normal combat. Therefore, he decided to fight him with the skill he had. He was very good at sling shots. He collected a few pebbles and took hold of his sling. Goliath did not know what the young boy was up to without a sword or armor. But he wanted to kill him anyway. When Goliath charged towards

Dāwūd, he put the pebbles on the sling and started whirling shots. These pebbles shot out of the sling at the speed of a bullet. One pebble hit Goliath on his forehead and a few others hit him on his face and eyes. Within minutes giant Goliath fell down on the ground, bleeding to his death.

Even the enemy could not believe Goliath would fall down within minutes. On seeing his fate, the enemy began to flee form the battleground. The Israelites chased them, captured them and killed all the soldiers. Years of suffering at the hands of the enemy ended.

Dāwūd becomes the king: Dāwūd became a hero overnight. Tālūt kept his word and married his daughter to Dāwūd. Several years later when Tālūt died, Dāwūd became the king of the Israelites.

From this story we learned that as long as we remain in the path of Allāh and struggle for a good cause, Allāh will help us. Tālūt's enemies were strong, but with Allāh's help Tālūt became victorious. Similarly we can become victorious in our struggle.

Even if we do not have any enemy, our daily life is full of struggle. We are trying hard to be good student, good Muslim, and good citizen. We are trying hard to avoid temptations, bad influences and bad friends. We have to win the struggle of our life. In order to win the struggle we need three things:

(a) perseverance,
(b) firm feet and
(c) help.

We should make it a point to learn the du'ā used by Tālūt and Dāwūd and pray to Allāh for victory in our life. With Allāh's help we can become victorious in our life.

Interesting Facts:

There are two types of slings. The slingshot is a Y-shaped structure, with an attached rubber band. Although rubber was available in Central and South America about 3,500 years back, it was not available in the Middle East at that time.

Dāwūd must have used the other type of sling, the shepherd's sling. Such slings have two pieces of cord, and a pouch in the center that holds the rock. To throw the rock, you have to swing the sling holding both the cords. The moment you release one cord, the rock shoots out.

Slings are types of projectile weapons. Dāwūd had used a better technology to fight against a strong enemy. Future projectile weapons include guns and cannons.

In the next few lessons, we will continue to see that Dāwūd was innovative and a technologically advanced person.

1. Memorize the du'ā of Tālūt and Dāwūd as mentioned in verse 2:250. Learn the meaning of the du'ā. Be ready to recite it in the next class.

2. Who announced that Tālūt would be the king of the Israelites?

    (a)   A nabi.
    (b)   Goliath.
    (c)   A poor man.
    (d)   The soldiers.

3. What are the three things Tālūt and Dāwūd prayed for before going out to war?

    (a)   Money, soldier and victory.
    (b)   Patience, strong foot and help.
    (c)   Patience, food and armor.
    (d)   Help, arms and strong army.

4. What was the reason Goliath refused to fight with Dāwūd?

    (a)   Dāwūd was a young boy.
    (b)   Dāwūd was more ferocious than Goliath.
    (c)   Dāwūd was a king.
    (d)   He was scared Dāwūd might kill him.

5. Dāwūd did not have the skill and strength like Goliath. But Dāwūd was not scared of him. Write in your own words why Dāwūd thought he was sure to win.

6. Search the index of an English translation of the Qur'ān by the word Tālūt or Jālūt. Then write down in which sūrah their story is narrated.

7. At the time of Tālūt, the Israelites were fighting against oppressors. Who were the oppressors?

    (a)   The Turkish tribes.
    (b)   The Egyptian tribes.
    (c)   The Chinese tribes.
    (d)   The Philistines.

Dāwūd (A) and Sulaimān (A)

Objective of the Lesson:

Dāwūd and Sulaimān were two father-and-son prophets in Islam. They were wise and knowledgeable kings. Their history shows prophets of Allāh were not always poor; some of them were powerful, rich and strong. This lesson discusses their life and achievements as narrated in the Qur'ān.

Dāwūd (A) and Sulaimān (A) are few of the father-and-son prophets mentioned in the Qur'ān. Other such prophets were Ibrāhīm and his two sons Ismā'īl and Ishāq; Ishāq and his son Ya'qūb; Ya'qūb and his son Yūsuf; and Zakariyyāh and his son Yahyā. Sometimes the mission started by a father was not finished in his lifetime. After the father passed away, the son took over from the father and continued preaching the words of Allāh to the people. The sons automatically did not become prophets because nobody can decide on their own to become prophets. Allāh appoints the prophets. The reason Allāh appointed the sons as prophets was because they were righteous people and they were capable of leading a community towards the right path.

In this lesson we will study about the many similarities between Dāwūd and Sulaimān.

Early history of Dāwūd: A long time back, Israelites lived in the valley of Canaan in ancient Palestine, which is now called Israel. In the previous lesson we learned that they were facing hostilities from Philistines. We also learned that young Dāwūd was able to destroy the fearsome Jālūt or Goliath. Later when Tālūt died, the Israelites appointed Dāwūd as their king.

Dāwūd becomes a prophet: All his life Dāwūd

was a righteous person. He believed in one Allāh and prayed to Him. He was a very persevering and hard working person. He used to sing beautiful songs praising glory of Allāh. Allāh appointed him as a prophet of the Israelites. Allāh revealed **Zabūr** to him. Zabūr is a divine book. He was not only a king of the Israelites, but also a prophet to guide them towards the right path. Allāh gave him wisdom and intelligence. He controlled the rebellious people and jinn under his rule. He made them work for him. They were employed to build king's palaces and develop the cities for the Israelites to live. Dāwūd was a very good judge. His way of justice was fair and proper. People used to come to him with all types of legal problems.

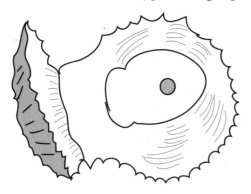

He used to solve the problems in a right manner. Later in this lesson we will study about one of his judgment mentioned in the Qur'ān.

Dāwūd was a skillful person. He learned the language of the birds and used birds in his army. He knew how to melt copper and iron. He used these metals to make armor for his army.

Sulaimān becomes a prophet: After Dāwūd passed away, one of his sons, Sulaimān, became the king of the Israelites. Allāh appointed Sulaimān as a prophet and gave him knowledge, wisdom and ability to do justice. Like his father, Sulaimān too was able to understand the language of the birds. He had a large number of horses in his army. He also used the birds in his army. He controlled the ferocious jinn and made them work in his empire. The jinn dived under the sea to get pearls for

Sulaimān. He also controlled the wind and made his ships sail to distant places.

As time passed by, Sulaimān became very rich. Yet he never forgot to pray to Allāh and submit to Him. He was kind hearted and gentle. His ability to do fair justice was extraordinary. During his rule, he conquered several countries. One such country was the Land of Saba. We shall learn about this land and its queen in the next lesson.

Story of fair judgment: The Qur'ān has narrated a story of fair judgment by Dāwūd and Sulaimān in sūrah Al-Anbiyā'.

When Dāwūd was still a king, a farmer and a shepherd came to him seeking judgment. The farmer told him that he had a field of crop. One night the shepherd's sheep entered the garden and destroyed the entire crop. He wanted the shepherd to pay for the damage, but the shepherd refused. Dāwūd listened to their case and then gave a judgment saying the shepherd should hand over his sheep to the farmer as payment for the lost crop.[21:78]

Sulaimān was listening to the judgment. He thought the ruling of the judgment could be made even better. He asked his father to change the ruling. He thought he could give a better sentence. He explained that garden was the capital of the farmer and sheep were capital of the shepherd. The word "capital" means the assets or the principal

amount. The farmer did not lose the capital but he lost the product that comes out of the capital. The land was the capital and the crop was the product.

The shepherd should not lose the capital but pay by the value of the product. Sulaimān suggested that the farmer should take care of the sheep temporarily and get all benefit out of the sheep. For example, he could use the hair for wool, milk for consumption, new-born baby sheep to keep for him etc. He would continue to use the "product" out of the sheep until the value of the lost crop was recovered. After that he would return the sheep to the original owner. Dāwūd realized this was a better judgment. He changed his previous ruling. Both the men were happy with this new judgment.

Interesting Facts:

Sulaimān may have used his divers to explore the bottom of the Red Sea and Mediterranean Sea. The average depth of the Red Sea is about 500 meters, while about 25% of this sea is less than 50 m deep.

At the center of the Red Sea is a trench of about 2500 m in depth.

Divers who dive without any breathing equipment are free divers. Current world records indicate that people can free dive to a depth of about 225 meters.

1. Read verse 2:251. What are the two things Allāh gave Dāwūd?

_____

2. Read verse 38:26. Allāh asked Dāwūd to do something and advised him not to do something. What were the two things?

to do: _____

not to do: _____

3. Read verse 4:163. What did Allāh give Dāwūd?

_____

4. Read verse 21:78. Dāwūd and Sulaimān gave a judgment about a case. What was the case about?

_____

_____

5. Find the words: SULAIMAN, DAWUD, GOLIATH, ZABUR, SAUL, TALUT, BILQIS, CANNAN, SLING, BIRD,

```
A  S  U  L  A  I  M  A  N
G  L  Z  D  W  B  I  R  D
O  I  A  E  D  A  W  U  D
L  N  B  I  L  Q  I  S  A
I  G  U  C  A  N  N  A  N
A  S  R  E  W  E  R  U  T
T  A  L  U  T  C  N  L  D
H  Z  S  R  O  P  A  B  M
```

Sulaimān (A) and the Queen

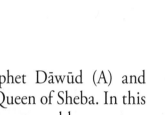

Objective of the Lesson:

The history of Sulaimān's interaction with the queen of Sheba is fascinating. It tells us about integrity and righteousness of Sulaimān. The students will learn the episode with the prophet and the queen.

In the previous lesson we learned about prophet Dāwūd (A) and Sulaimān (A). We also briefly discussed about Queen of Sheba. In this lesson we will study additional details about the queen and her contacts with prophet Sulaimān. In the Qur'ān, the story of the Queen of Sheba is discussed in detail in sūrah an-Naml, sūrah number 27. There is another sūrah named after the kingdom of Sheba. The name of the sūrah is as-Saba', sūrah number 34. This sūrah briefly mentions that the kingdom was made a sign for the people.

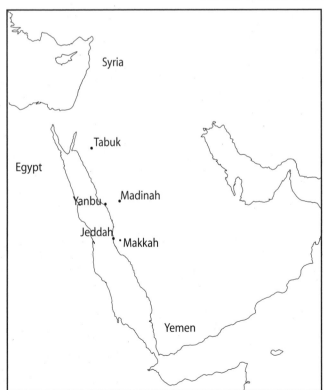

Location of Sheba: Although the Qur'ān does not mention its location, the traditional Islamic sources believe the kingdom of Sheba was located in Yemen. However, most of the biblical reports and ancient African legends indicate the kingdom was located somewhere in Ethiopia. Some of the recent archeological findings indicate the kingdom was probably located in the Northwest Arabia. According to these findings Sheba was a prosperous trading center in that region.

The Queen of Sheba: The kingdom of Sheba was ruled by various kings and at least one queen. We do not know about other kings, but the Qur'ān has mentioned about its queen. Her name is not mentioned in the Qur'ān, but the historical report indicate that she was Bilqis, a successful ruler.

Sūrah an-Naml provides interesting details about the queen. Her throne was magnificent.[27:23] It had detailed work of fine design. It was decorated with faces and images of idols. The people in her country worshipped the sun.[27:24] She was probably a sun worshipper.

Just as our president has several secretaries to advise him about the government, Bilqis too had a group of people to advise her. She consulted them whenever it was needed.[27:32]

Sulaimān came to know about Sheba: Sulaimān had a vast kingdom. He conquered many nations, but not the rich nation of Sheba. One day he was inspecting his army. His army consisted of foot soldiers, chariots, cavalry, horses and birds. The birds were used to carry secret messages from one place to the other. The messengers used to write down messages, tie it on the bird's feet and let the bird carry the message to and from the king. During the inspection of the army, Sulaimān noticed one of his important birds was missing. He said if the bird did not show up on time, he would punish it.

The bird flew back from Sheba. Sulaimān came to know from the bird that there was a kingdom called Sheba, ruled by a queen. He learned about her great throne,[27:23] and the sun worshippers. These people were worshipping the sun because shaitān had misguided them away from worshipping Allāh.[27:24]

Sulaimān sent letters to the queen: Sulaimān

decided to send a letter to the queen. The bird carried the letter back to Sheba. The queen, surprised to receive the letter, called her advisors: *"O my chiefs! I received a noble letter. The letter is from Sulaimān. It reads: In the name of Allāh, the most merciful, most kind."*

She further read: *Do not go against me, but come to me as a Muslim.*[27:31]

Bilqis set up a meeting with her advisors. They worked on a strategy. They knew that their kingdom was fairly strong.[27:33] It was probably possible for them to defend the country if Sulaimān attacked it. Bilqis knew it was a serious situation. She was also surprised at the content of the letter, which carried an invitation to change their faith. She did not know what exactly to expect from Sulaimān. In her mind, she thought, Sulaimān might actually be looking for wealth. She knew that strong kings invade countries, destroy the towns and take all the people as prisoners.[27:34] She wanted to avoid a war.

Bilqis sent a gift: In response to the letter she decided to send Sulaimān a valuable gift. The Qur'ān does not say what gift she sent. It was probably a valuable gift that a king can give to another king. When Sulaimān received the gift, he was angry. He did not want the gift. Allāh had given him lots of wealth. He said: *"What Allāh has given me is better than that which He has given you."*[27:36] Sulaimān refused to accept the gift and told the messenger who carried the gift: *"You enjoy in your gift."* Then he told him: *"Go back to them. We shall surely come to them with large army and they cannot resist. We shall drive them out of the country with shame and we shall lower their dignity."*[27:37]

Queen's throne: After the messenger left, Sulaimān asked that someone should bring him the queen's throne. He wanted the queen's throne brought to him before the queen surrendered to him. A strong jinn volunteered to bring the throne. When the throne was brought to him, Sulaimān was impressed at its beauty and value. He was not tempted to keep the expensive throne. He knew his goal was to spread the messages of Allāh. He told his people to change the throne to test if Bilqis could recognize it.

Queen arrives: After a few days, the queen arrived at Sulaimān's palace. Sulaimān showed her the throne that she had owned. It was the same throne but he changed it. She had no idea her

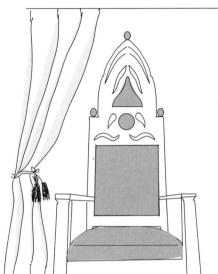

throne was brought over to Sulaimān's palace. She looked at the throne and said: *"As though it was the same."*[27:42]

The purpose of changing the throne was probably to make her realize that power and strength are not permanent, these can be changed. She thought her power was permanent,[27:43] therefore she did not accept Islam after receiving the letter from Sulaimān.[27:29] Her pride made her stubborn.

Then Sulaimān asked the queen to enter the palace. The palace was unique in many ways. It had large glass slabs placed over flowing water. When someone looked at the water, they could not tell a glass slab was on top of the water. When Bilqis stepped into the palace she thought her skirt would get wet. She lifted her skirt slightly, but to her astonishment, her feet did not touch the water. She realized that she was fooled by the appearance of the glass slab. She also realized that she had always been fooled by the glitter of this world, and could not see the Truth.

Bilqis realized she was wrong not to worship Allāh. She admitted she was wrong when she worshipped the sun. She accepted Islam and submitted to Allāh—the Lord of all the worlds.

Interesting Facts:

We do not surely know the types of birds used by Sulaimān in sending his messages. However, homing pigeons were used in many countries to transfer messages from one place to another.

The homing pigeons can travel about 1000 miles in two days at an average speed of 30 miles an hour. They can travel short distances at a speed of 60 mph, almost as fast as a car on an expressway.

During World War I, a homing pigeon received a bravery award from the French Army.

Tipu Sultan, a Muslim king in India, had a large collection of homing pigeons for his army.

Dāwūd (A) had learned the technology to melt iron.[34:10] His kingdom was technologically advanced and could use the iron to make armors.[34:11]

Melting iron requires furnaces that can produce high temperature. Similar high temperature is also needed for glass making. For making glass slabs, large furnaces are needed to melt huge amount of silica. Under Sulaimān's rule, the technology of furnaces continued to develop. Bilqis most likely was not aware of such a technology.

The earliest glass slab was excavated in Beth She'arim, a place once ruled by Sulaimān. This glass lab weighs about 18,000 pounds and measures 6.5 x 11 feet.

homework**weekend 11**

1. Which sūrah in the Qur'ān has detailed account of the kingdom of Sheba and its queen?

   (a)   Sūrah Saba'
   (b)   Sūrah an-Naml
   (c)   Sūrah Baqarah
   (d)   Sūrah Maryam

2.   Based on what you have read about the kingdom of Sheba in the lesson, where do you think it was located?

   (a)   South of Saudi Arabia
   (b)   North of Iraq
   (c)   West of Egypt
   (d)   Near ancient Iran

3. Read verse 27:24. Who were worshipping the sun?

_____

4. Sulaimān sent a letter to the queen of Sheba. What was the first sentence of the letter? Read verse 27:30 to answer.

_____

5. What did Sulaimān do when he received a gift from the queen of Sheba?

   (a)   He liked it very much and kept it.
   (b)   He broke the gift into pieces.
   (c)   He donated the gift to a local mosque.
   (d)   He refused to accept the gift.

Mūsā (A) and Fir'awn

Objective of the Lesson:

Interaction between Fir'awn and Mūsā (A) started when Mūsā was an infant and it lasted until the death of Fir'awn. It was a long history of ups and down, trust and suspicion, power struggle and righteousness. This lesson summarizes the highlights of their interaction with each other and provides a platform from which we can learn additional dynamics about the mission of Mūsā.

In this lesson we will study about the life and activities of Mūsā (A) and Fir'awn as narrated in the Qur'ān. The purpose of this study is to take a brief look at the life of Mūsā in Egypt and Madyan and understand important turning points in his life. We studied briefly about Mūsā in a previous lesson (**Promise of Allāh**, Lesson 2) in this book. Let us develop the story from that chapter.

Childhood: a miracle of Allāh: In Lesson 2 we mentioned Fir'awn had ordered to kill all male children of the Israelites and let the female children live.

We had learned that Mūsā was picked up from a basket floating in the river. The wife of Fir'awn had adopted baby Mūsā as her son. We also learned that Mūsā lived in Fir'awn's palace under the care of his own mother. Fir'awn wanted to kill all new born male babies of the Israelites. If the above incident had not happened, Fir'awn would have killed baby Mūsā. But due to Allāh's master plan, things took a different turn!

Mūsā as a young adult: Mūsā grew up in the palace of Fir'awn as a prince. But his princely upbringing ended soon.

When he was a young man one day he noticed an Egyptian and an Israelite were fighting on the street.[28:15] He tried to stop their quarrel. He hit the Egyptian with a hard blow, but the man died from the blow. Later someone told him Fir'awn was planning to punish Mūsā with death. Mūsā knew he would not get justice, therefore he ran

away from the country. Thus, all of a sudden the future course of life changed. From being a prince in Fir'awn's palace, overnight he became a fugitive—running for his life.

Mūsā becomes a prophet: Mūsā ran away from Egypt towards **Madyan**, a place east of Egypt. He got married there and settled down. Several years later Allāh appointed Mūsā as a prophet. Allāh gave Mūsā two signs—when he threw his rod, it turned into a snake and when he pulled his hand from his bosom, it turned white.[7:106-108] Allāh then instructed Mūsā to return to Egypt to give guidance to Fir'awn and his people because they became very bad people.[28:32] Mūsā was also told to rescue the Israelites because they were suffering in Egypt. Mūsā was worried to return because he thought Fir'awn might punish him for the old crime of killing an Egyptian. But Allāh assured him that nothing would happen to him.

Return to Egypt: Mūsā returned to Egypt with his brother Hārūn. Mūsā had a stammering problem; he was not good at speech. However, Hārūn was an excellent speaker. Both of them went to Fir'awn's court. They had a lengthy debate with Fir'awn about the oneness of Allāh and told him to release the Israelites from their slavery.

Fir'awn's response: Fir'awn used to tell his people that he was god. Obviously he did not like what Mūsā was telling him about Allāh. He teased

Mūsā and tried to make everybody laugh at him. He said if Mūsā was a prophet of God, why did he look so poor? Why did he not have good clothes? He jokingly told everybody to build a big tower for him so that he can climb the tower and take a look at Mūsā's Allāh.[28:38] Then he asked Mūsā what proof did he bring with him about his claim. Mūsā showed the two signs—the one about the rod turning into a snake and his hand turning white. Yet Fir'awn was not satisfied. He wanted people to believe that Mūsā was only a magician. Mūsā told him he was not a magician because magicians cannot be successful.[10:81]

Fir'awn thought he could find good magicians from his country to prove that they were better than Mūsā. He sent people to find good magicians from far off places. These magicians were hoping for generous rewards for a good magic show. Fir'awn arranged a big festivity. A large number of people gathered to see the show.

The magicians cast their ropes and rods and created awesome magic in the eyes of the audience. Then Allāh inspired Mūsā to cast his rod. His rod

turned into a snake and started to swallow all those that the magicians made up. Now the magicians were helpless. They fell down on the ground and bowed to Allāh. They accepted Islam and believed in Mūsā as the prophet of Allāh.

More Signs by Mūsā: Mūsā stayed in Egypt for few more years. His job was not yet done. He still could not guide Fir'awn and could not make the Israelites free from slavery. Allāh wanted to give Fir'awn more opportunity to come to the right path. He gave Mūsā more signs. In total there were **nine signs** sent to Mūsā.[7:133] These signs were rod, hand, lice, blood, epidemic, frog, locust, famine and loss of fruits. Except the rod and hand, other seven signs caused disaster in Egypt. For example, when locusts swarmed the country, they ate away the crop, as a result there was famine, the next sign. When lice appeared, it created an epidemic and people started dying. Each time a tragedy happened, Fir'awn told Mūsā to pray to Allāh to remove the tragedy. He promised if the tragedy was removed, then he would believe in Allāh. Each time Allāh removed the tragedy, Fir'awn did not believe, but became a bigger disbeliever.

Fir'awn's end nears: Allāh always gives the sinners enough time to correct their mistake and come back to the right path. Fir'awn was given enough time year after year to return to the right path, but he did not.

Allāh told Mūsā to take the Israelites out of Egypt one night. Rescuing the Israelites meant Fir'awn's time was up. Mūsā told thousands of Israelites to walk out of Egypt by night. Next morning Fir'awn was angry to find that he had no slaves! A kingdom as big as his cannot function without the cheap labors. He and his army chased the Israelites. By that time, Mūsā had already brought the Israelites to the edge of a sea. By the grace of Allāh Mūsā struck a dry path.[20:77] The Israelites crossed the sea by the dry path and moved to the other side. Fir'awn thought he could also cross the sea, but as soon as he came in the middle of the path, the water in the sea rushed and drowned him. While dying in the sea water Fir'awn realized he had no chance of surviving. At the last minute he said he believed in God of Mūsā.[10:90] Allāh said such last minute acceptance would not help him.

From the summarized account we learned both Mūsā and Fir'awn affected each other's course of life. Mūsā's destiny was good because he trusted Allāh and he was righteous. Fir'awn's destiny was destruction because he did not believe in Allāh and he terrorized his people.

1. Read verse 28:7. What two things Allāh told Mūsā's mother in the verse.

_____

Based on the same verse what two things Allāh promises He would do?

_____

2. Read verse 28:27. After Mūsā got married in Madyan, how many years was he expected to live in the place?

_____

3. Read verse 7:128. Mūsā told his people to do two things. What are the two things he told his people to do or follow?

(a) _____ (b) _____

4. Read verse 7:133. The verse speaks of some of the signs of Allāh. Mention the signs below:

(a) _____ (b) _____ (c) _____

(d) _____ (e) _____

5. Read verse 69 sūrah Tā Hā. Who will never be successful? Explain why they will not be successful.

_____

_____

Bani Isrā'īl: *Life After Their Rescue*

Objective of the Lesson:

The history of Bani Isrā'īl after their rescue is full of trials, sufferings, trust, betrayal, misguidance and guidance. Bani Isrā'īl received Allāh's blessing throughout their history, but they also rebelled against Allāh. This lesson summarizes their history after their rescue from Egypt, when they became disobedient to Mūsā (A) and started many types of wrongdoings.

The history of Bani Isrā'īl after their rescue from Egypt carries a deep wisdom. Many verses and several sūrah in the Qur'ān talk about this history. The history has dramatic turns and carries a moral lesson for everybody. The Qur'ān has not narrated the history to entertain us, but to make us learn from the trials and mistakes of others. Let us study some of the key events of the history as narrated in the Qur'ān.

In the Qur'ān Allāh says he had favored Bani Isrā'īl because they were oppressed by Pharaoh and his people.[2:47; 2:122] During the time of Pharaoh, the ruler used to kill the male children of Bani Isrā'īl and let the females live.[2:49; 7:141] The Israelites were treated as second class citizen without having any civil rights and status. They lived under extreme hardship. In order to rescue them from the suffering, Allāh sent prophet Mūsā to guide and establish them as a free nation. Accordingly Mūsā brought them across the sea and gave them freedom. Our story begins here—after the Israelites were rescued.

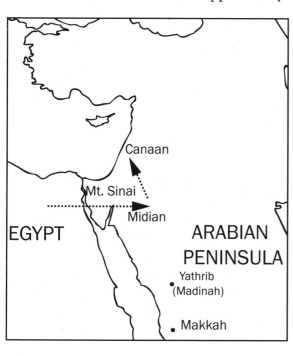

Mūsā went for meditation: Mūsā rescued thousands of Bani Isrā'īl from Egypt across the sea and brought them in Midian or Madyan, a region north of Arabia. His eventual goal was to take them to the land of **Canaan** in ancient Palestine. Allāh promised them the land would be theirs as a token of gift. Allāh wanted to establish them as a nation and bless them with His mercy.

Soon after Mūsā rescued Bani Isrā'īl, he went to **Mount Sinai**. He used to receive divine guidance from Allāh in the mountain. He thought Allāh would give him further guidance about how to

lead the nation of Israelites. Before leaving for the mountain, he appointed his brother Hārūn to be the leader of Bani Isrā'īl.

Bani Isrā'īl became rebellious: During the absence of Mūsā, Bani Isrā'īl began to ignore Hārūn. Their faith in Allāh quickly disappeared. They began to feel homesick about their life in Egypt, although it was full of suffering and torture. They were still under the influence of Egyptian mentality. In Egypt they saw the king and the people worshipped idols. They began asking Hārūn to set up an idol for them to worship. Hārūn would not listen because he was a prophet of Allāh. How could he tell them to worship idols?

There were a few people among them who showed them how they could make their own idols. While escaping from Egypt, the Bani Isrā'īl had brought some gold and jewelry. They melted the gold and made a golden calf to worship it as their god. The calf was hollow inside. When wind blew over the calf, it used to make a sound. Sūrah Baqarah in the Qur'ān is named after this episode. The word Baqarah means the calf.

Mūsā's disappointment: When Mūsā was in the mountain, he received divine revelations called the **Ten Commandments.** These commandments were the guiding principles for the Israelites. Mūsā returned from the mountain with great hope to guide the people but he was shocked and surprised to find they were worshipping an idol. He first became angry with Hārūn thinking that he allowed them to build the calf and worship it. Hārūn told him that he was helpless with these rebellious people. They did not listen to him. Then Mūsā asked the people to break the idol and seek forgiveness of Allāh. Bani Isrā'īl felt sorry for starting idol worshipping.

Promised land remains a distant hope: Mūsā did not want Bani Isrā'īl to remain in wilderness. He wanted them to own the Promised Land. The land was in Canaan. At that time it was occupied by the ferocious **Amelikite** people. The Amelikites were idol worshippers. Allāh wanted to punish them at the hands of Bani Isrā'īl. But to occupy the land Bani Isrā'īl needed planning and preparations.

Mūsā selected a few people to go and spy upon the Amelikites and bring information. These people went for spying but came back with bad news. They thought the Amelikites were like giants and very ferocious. They believed there was no way they could defeat the Amelikites. They refused to invade Canaan even after Mūsā repeatedly asked them to invade. Mūsā was frustrated with his

people for not listening to his advice. Even though Allāh assured them Canaan would be theirs, they did not trust Allāh or Mūsā. They were a rebellious people.

Mūsā was disappointed with his people. He cursed them and told them they deserved to remain like vagabonds for forty long years.[5:26] As a result of not listening to Allāh, Bani Isrā'īl remained

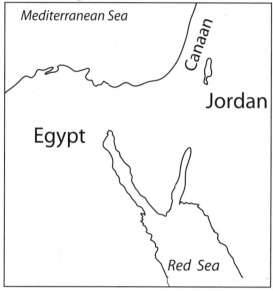

in wilderness for nearly one whole generation. Ultimately after forty years of aimless life, they finally occupied Canaan, but by that time Mūsā had passed away.

Examples of other rebellion: The Qur'ān has mentioned many examples of rebellion by Bani Isrā'īl. Allāh had favored them and chose them above other nations of that time, but they refused to listen to Allāh. They accepted Mūsā as their spiritual leader but continued to annoy him.[33:69] They were a greedy nation. Allāh gave them Manna and Salwa as food to eat during their life in wilderness.[2:57; 7:160] However, they became tired of the food. They wanted fruits and vegetables like those they used to eat in Egypt.[2:61] They wanted to go back to Egypt. Mūsā could not make them understand that the freedom was much better than slavery in Egypt.

After Mūsā passed away, Bani Isrā'īl made changes to their divine book. They deleted parts of the book and added new things in the book. They received many other prophets to guide them, but often rejected them. They were told to preserve the honor of Sabbath—the Jewish holiday when nobody works. But they violated Sabbath. They oppressed the poor and charged high interest money from others.

Due to ignoring the divine message, refusing to believe in the prophets, making changes in the divine book and overall corruption, the Bani Isrā'īl was condemned by Allāh. They were punished by Allāh many times.

We should learn lessons from their history. As long as we remain in the right path, Allāh will always bless us. If we move away from the path of Allāh, we will suffer punishment and disaster.

1. Read verse 2:55. It gives us an example about rebellion of the Israelites. What did the Israelites wanted to see?

_____

2. In verse 2:59, the Qur'ān says Israelites did something wrong. What did they do?

_____

3. Read verse 2:61 As a result of constant arrogance and rebellion, something happened to the Israelites. What happened to them?

_____

4. Due to refusal to occupy the Holy Land, it was banned for the Israelites for a certain number of years. How many years was it banned for them?

    (a)   100 years.
    (b)   50 years.
    (c)   40 years.
    (d)   10 years.

5. The Qur'ān says the Israelites were given two good foods during their life in the wilderness. What were the foods?

    (a)   Sabbath.
    (b)   Mann and Salwa.
    (c)   Camel and goat.
    (d)   Cucumber and pomegranate.

6. When the Children of Israel continued their rebellion, at one point they were turned in to something. Read verse 7:166 and select the correct choice below.

    (a) They became swine, despised and killed.
    (b) They became worms, creepy and ugly.
    (c) They became like apes, despised and rejected.
    (d) They became slaves, punished and humiliated.

Mūsā (A) and Khidir

Objective of the Lesson:

The travel of Mūsā (A) and Khidir was full of dramatic events which have deep meaning. This lesson narrates the three incidents that happened during their travel, and emphasizes that our knowledge is extremely small compared to the knowledge of Allāh.

The Qur'ān has a beautiful story about Mūsā (A) and Khidir, narrated in sūrah Al-Kahf. No historical person was identified with Khidir. According to some, he was a saint, while others view him as a prophet. Everybody agrees he was a wise person. Mūsā trusted him and wanted to gain knowledge from him.[18:66]

Mūsā meets Khidir: Like the learned people of the past, once Mūsā traveled to far off places in search of knowledge.[18:60] During this travel, he met a person whose name was Khidir. Mūsā wanted to follow him to gain knowledge. Khidir told him in order to gain knowledge he will require patience. He was afraid Mūsā might not have patience.[18:67] Mūsā assured him that he would be patient. They made an agreement that Mūsā would not ask any questions during the travel until Khidir explains everything.

Story 1: The boat: During the travel they encountered three different events. The first event happened when they boarded a boat. Khidir purposely made a hole on the boat. Mūsā was surprised to see Khidir's conduct. He asked Khidir why did he damage the boat, now it would drown with the people on board. Mūsā further told him that it was a bad on his part to turn a good boat useless. In reply Khidir reminded Mūsā about their agreement. Mūsā had agreed that he would not ask any question and not loose his patience. Mūsā felt sorry for asking question, but he was remained very surprised.

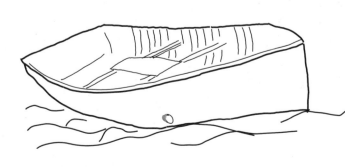

Story 2: The boy: Mūsā continued to follow Khidir. They traveled to another place where Khidir met a boy.[18:74] Surprisingly, Khidir killed the boy. Seeing this incredible act, Mūsā forgot about his promise. He asked why he killed an innocent boy. Mūsā thought it was a very bad thing to do.

Once again Khidir reminded Mūsā about their agreement. Mūsā was not supposed to ask any question or loose his patience. Khidir was disappointed with him. He reminded Mūsā if he asked any other question after this, they would stop traveling together. Obviously Mūsā did not want to end the travel. Therefore he tried to keep his patience, but in his heart he could not support all the things Khidir was doing.

Story 3: The wall: After a long travel, Mūsā and Khidir reached a town. Both of them were hungry. The people of the town were miser, they refused to give them any food. As Mūsā and Khidir were crossing the town, they found a wall about to collapse. Khidir started to repair the wall. Mūsā was surprised at this. He thought these people of the town refused to give them food, yet Khidir repaired their damaged wall. If he wanted, he could have taken a salary from them,

with which he could have purchased some food. The moment Mūsā expressed his thoughts, Khidir became angry.

Khidir knew Mūsā would fail to be patient. Yet he allowed Mūsā to accompany him because they had an agreement. Now Khidir told Mūsā they could not travel together anymore, they must separate. However, before separating, He explained the reasons behind each of his actions.

The explanations: The explanations of the events show Mūsā's knowledge was limited. He knew things in the present, but he did not know the future. Mūsā knew only those things that he could see and understand. Therefore, according to Mūsā, damaging the boat and killing the boy were evil actions. Under ordinary knowledge anybody would conclude these were bad actions.

However, only if we could see the future, we would be able to tell if a particular action is good or bad. Khidir had the knowledge about the future. He was acting based on the knowledge given by Allāh. Even though the boat owner would be unhappy to see the damage, in the long run he would be happier. A local king was forcefully collecting all good boats for a war. The king would have collected this boat also, but he would not take a boat with a hole. The poor boat owner would fix it later and continue to use it for fishing.

Death of a child would make his parents sad,

but Khidir knew there were blessings behind the death. If this boy lived, he would grow up and torture his parents. Allāh would give the parents another boy who would grow up to be obedient to them.

Underneath the damaged wall was a treasure that belonged to two orphans. Their dead father was a good man. Khidir wanted the orphans to grow up and then find the treasure. Therefore he repaired the wall free of charge as a kindness towards the orphans.

The actions that seemed cruel, were actually full of kindness and mercy.

What we learn from these stories: In our life, sometimes bad things happen. We feel sad about it. We wish the bad thing had not happened. If we trust Allāh, we may one day realize that something good came out from a bad incident. Sometimes we may never realize. Allāh has the ultimate knowledge. He does things in a certain manner that we do not always understand. We must trust Allāh and remember that we do not have the knowledge to understand everything. As long as we are righteous, in the long run all hardship in our life will have a blessing in them.

Sometimes when bad things happen to us we ask, 'Allāh, why did you make me suffer,' or we say, 'Allāh I always pray, fast and give zakāt yet why did you give me this suffering.' We should not forget that Allāh has a master plan for us. He does things in the best interest for us. Sometimes He tests us with fear, hunger, loss of lives, loss of crops etc., but those who persevere under trying conditions ultimately become successful. [2:155-157]

If you look at the life of the Prophet (S) you will get similar lessons. The Prophet (S) had to abandon his homeland and migrate to Madīnah. There was certainly a Master Plan from Allāh about the life of the Prophet (S) and future of the Muslims. Eventually the migration helped the Prophet establish the religion of Islam as the driving force. Islam became a way of life for not only entire Arabia, but also for the billions of people in the world.

1. What explanation did Khidir give for damaging the boat?

    (a)   It belonged to the king and Khidir did not want him to have a boat.
    (b)   The king would capture all good boats, but not the bad boats.
    (c)   It belonged to two orphans who would use it later.
    (d)   It belonged to people who did not help the hungry people.

2. What was the reason Khidir killed the boy?

    (a)   The boy would grow up and become a bad king.
    (b)   The boy would grow up and hurt the orphans.
    (c)   The boy would grow up and hurt his parents.
    (d)   The boy would grow up and become obedient.

3. Even though the people of the town did not give Khidir food, why did he repair their damaged wall?

    (a)   To get some money in return.
    (b)   To teach them a lesson for their rudeness.
    (c)   To preserve the treasure for the two orphans.
    (d)   To take a share of the treasure underneath the wall.

4. What was Mūsā required to do for traveling with Khidir?

    _____

5. What was the reason Mūsā wanted to travel with Khidir?

    (a)   To gain money.
    (b)   To gain knowledge.
    (c)   To become a prophet.
    (d)   To meet Fir'awn.

6. (a) In which sūrah is the story of Khidir and Mūsā related? (b) Where was the sūrah revealed?

    (a) _____ (b) _____

'Isā (A) and Maryam (ra)

Objective of the Lesson:

The history of 'Isā (A) and his mother Maryam is narrated in many different sūrahs. This lesson describes the key events and key issues in their life and mission as narrated in the Qur'ān.

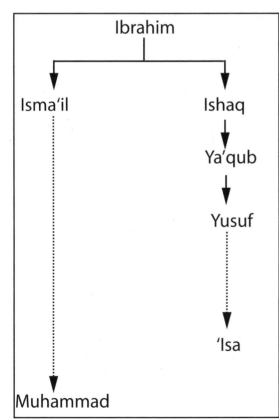

About six hundred years before our dear Prophet Muhammad (S) was born, prophet 'Isā (A) came to teach the unity of God. He came as a prophet to the followers of Mūsā (A). These followers were called Bani Isrā'īl or the Children of Israel. 'Isā was a prophet for the Children Israelites. In comparison Muhammad (S) is the prophet for the whole mankind. In this lesson we will study primarily about 'Isā and also about Maryam as narrated in the Qur'ān.

Ancestor of 'Isā: From the offspring of prophet Ibrāhīm (A) many prophets were chosen. His two sons, Ismā'īl and Ishāq, were prophets. From the offspring of Ismā'īl, the only prophet was Muhammad (S). From the offspring of Ishāq, many prophets came. The last prophet among them was 'Isā (A). He was also the last prophet of the Children of Israel.

Birth of 'Isā: The Qur'ān has discussed very little or nothing at all about the birth of most of the prophets. A short description is available about the birth of Yahyā. Similar short description is mentioned about the childhood of Mūsā. Nothing is mentioned about the birth of any other prophet except 'Isā. From the Qur'ān we find that 'Isā was born in a noble family. His mother was Maryam (ra) who was given a status over all other women in the world.[3:42] When Maryam was a young woman, angels brought her the message that a boy would be born to her.[3:45] She was surprised because she was unmarried and she was not a woman of bad character.[3:47; 19:20] Allāh informed her that even then a boy would be born. The boy was a *kalīmah* of Allāh.[3:45; 4:171] The word *kalīmah* means 'sign' or 'word' of Allāh. Maryam and her son was made a sign for the mankind.[19:21; 23:50] The angels brought a rūh for Maryam so that she can have a baby.[21:91]

After Maryam was carrying a baby, she moved to an eastern place.[19:22] Several months later when it was time to give birth to the child, Maryam sat down by the trunk of a date tree. Allāh revealed to her not to cry but to hold the date tree and shake it. It would drop ripe dates.[19:25] When ʿIsā was born, Allāh told her to eat the dates and be glad to see the child.

Maryam returns after childbirth: After the birth of ʿIsā, Maryam returned to her native land.[19:27] When the elderly people saw them they became angry. Earlier all the people loved her when she served in the temple, but now nobody liked her. They charged her:

"O Maryam! Why are you a rebel to the society? Your family is such a good family. This is not appropriate for you and your family!"

Maryam did not say a word but pointed at ʿIsā. He replied saying he was a prophet of Allāh and he was given a book. He was instructed to perform the salāt and give the zakāt. He was blessed the day he was born, the day he would die and the day he would be raised up.[19:30-33]

Mission of ʿIsā: ʿIsā was sent as a prophet for the Children of Israel to guide them and bring them to the path of righteousness.[3:49] One of the missions of ʿIsā was to confirm the previous scripture **Tawrāt** and bring additional guidance for the Children of Israel.[3:50] The new guidance was **Injīl**. Many people think Injīl is the Gospel—the four books in the Bible. The present day Gospel is not the original Injīl revealed by Allāh.

ʿIsā was helped by the Holy Spirit—**rūhul quddus**, which means angel Jibril (A). The Holy Spirit is not a god but an angel. Jibril had supported all other prophets who received the message from Allāh (swt). He helped ʿIsā by bringing the divine revelation to him.

Teachings of ʿIsā: The Qurʾān and the Bible mention many teachings of ʿIsā. The Qurʾān says ʿIsā taught his people to perform salāt and pay zakāt.[19:31] He taught them to worship none other than Allāh.[3:51] Even the Bible says that Jesus told his people to worship none but One God.

Followers of ʿIsā: The followers of ʿIsā were called **hawarriyun**.[61:14] He had very few followers. He used parables to speak to his followers. The

Children of Israel gave him hard time.

The history of all the prophets tells us that it was difficult to uphold the Truth. All the prophets faced extreme difficulty, but they never gave up the Truth. Ultimately, the Truth wins; therefore we

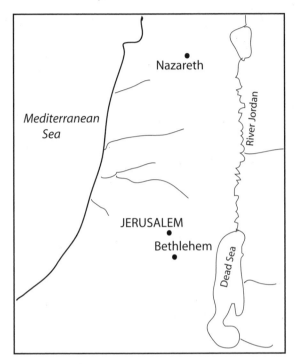

should never give up the Truth even if it appears difficult.

Unique abilities of 'Isā: The Qur'ān mentioned many unique abilities of 'Isā. He talked in the cradle and when he had grey hair.[3:46; 5:110] He had the ability to heal the blindness of his community. He made birds from clay and blew life in them.[3:49]

Attempt to kill 'Isā: The Children of Israel became enemies of 'Isā. They did not like his teachings. They planned to kill him. However, Allāh planned something else.[3:54] Allāh's plan is the best of all plans. The Qur'ān says they wanted to kill 'Isā but they could neither crucify him nor kill him.[4:157] Allāh raised him to Himself. [3:55; 4:158]

Son of God theory: The Children of Israel rejected 'Isā altogether. They accused him of being a fraud and did not accept his teachings. But over the years the Romans and Greeks began to like the teachings of 'Isā. These teachings were translated in Greek and Latin languages. Many of the non-Israelites also began to like the teachings. At that time they formed the religion of Christianity in the name of Christ or Jesus. 'Isā did not preach Christianity or any religion in his name. The new followers of Jesus began to say he was the Son of God. The Qur'ān strongly rejects the Son of God theory.

Position of 'Isā in Islam: In Islam the position of 'Isā is very high. Muslims respect both him and his mother. They consider him as a true prophet of Allāh. The Qur'ān says he was no more than a messenger.[4:171; 5:75] Muslims believe that the Injīl was revealed to him. Muslims do not celebrate Christmas—which the Christians think is the birthday of Jesus.

As with all other prophets, Allāh (swt) had blessed 'Isā (A). The Qur'ān mentions 'Isā (A) as **Masih** or the blessed one.

1. Read Sūrah Maryam, verse 36. According to ʿĪsā (A), what is the Right Path?

    _____

2. Read Sūrah Al-Hadīd (The Iron), verse 27. Then answer the following:

    a. What was given to ʿĪsā? _____

    b. What was given to the people who followed him? _____

3. Read Sūrah Az-Zukhruf (Sūrah 43) verse 59. To which community was ʿĪsā (A) sent?

    _____

4. Read As-Saff, verse 61:6. Answer the following based on the verse:

    a. Which Book did ʿĪsā (A) confirm? _____

    b. ʿĪsā (A) foretold the coming of which prophet? _____

5. Based on 61:14, Who believed in ʿĪsā (A) and who did not? What happened to those who believed him?

    a. _____

    b. _____

6. Read 19:31. What religious duties were enjoined upon ʿĪsā (A)?

    _____

7. Read Sūrah Maryam, verse 35. How does Allāh (swt) make something happen?

    _____

Khadījah (ra): *Finest Example of a Committed Wife*

Objective of the Lesson:

The students will learn about Khadījah (ra), the first wife of the Prophet (S). Her married life with the Prophet (S) reveals the qualities of this great woman. The lesson also sheds light on the life of Muhammad (S) before and after he became a prophet of Allāh.

In this lesson we will learn about Khadījah bint Khuwaylid, the first wife of Prophet Muhammad (S). She was also the first person to accept Islam from Muhammad (S). In a book of Hadīth it is narrated that the Prophet (S) had said Khadījah was one of the four best women in the world. She was also fondly called as **Khadījatul Kubrā** i.e. "Khadījah the Great." Her greatness comes from her dedication to Islam and support for her husband during the most difficult times of his life.

Khadījah was born in the year 555 C.E. She was known as bint Khuwaylid or daughter of Khuwaylid. She belonged to the Quraish tribe, under the clan of **Banu Asad**. A tribe is a bigger unit in a society; and under a tribe there can be many clans. A clan is group of people who are closely tied into a bigger family. For example, Banu Quraish was the tribe. Under the tribe there were many clans, such as Banu Hashim, Banu Nawfal, Banu Shams, etc.

Early life: Khadījah belonged to a business family. When Khadījah was ten years old, her mother died. When she was twenty years old her father died. Her father was a successful merchant in Arabia. After her

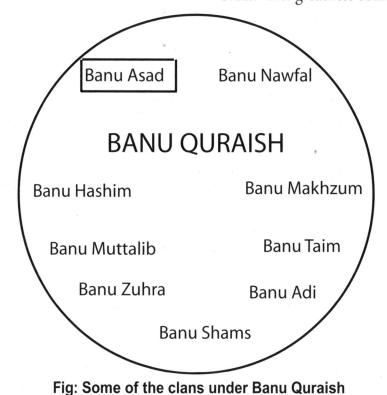

Banu Asad

Banu Nawfal

BANU QURAISH

Banu Hashim

Banu Makhzum

Banu Muttalib

Banu Taim

Banu Zuhra

Banu Adi

Banu Shams

Fig: Some of the clans under Banu Quraish

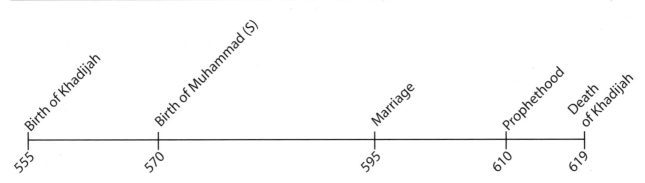

Birth of Khadījah — 555
Birth of Muhammad (S) — 570
Marriage — 595
Prophethood — 610
Death of Khadījah — 619

father died, Khadījah inherited all the property. She continued to do the trade of her father. She used to send caravans to Syria during the summer, and to Yemen during the winter. The trades used to bring her big profits. With these profits she used to feed and clothe the poor and help her relatives. She was married twice, and both her husbands died in tribal battles.

Employing Muhammad (S): Khadījah never traveled with her trade caravan. She used to send an agent to trade on her behalf. During one such trade to Syria she needed a reliable person. She knew about a young man named Muhammad (S), who had earned a nickname of **al-Amin** or The Trustworthy. She decided to employ him although he did not have any business experience. She knew that his lack of experience would be balanced by his trustworthiness. During the trade she also sent her reliable servant **Maysarah** to watch Muhammad (S).

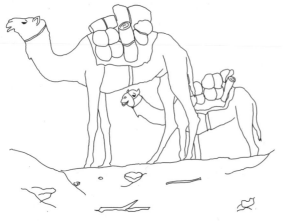

Return from the trade: As Muhammad (S) conducted trade in Syria, Maysarah continuously watched him as to how he conducted the business and how he dealt with the people. He was amazed to find Muhammad (S) was keeping track of every account honestly and sincerely. He did not try to cheat his employer. When they returned from the trade, Muhammad (S) submitted to Khadījah the entire income from the trade. He explained the details of the business trade and accounted for every coin. Khadījah was very impressed with his honesty and hardworking nature. She found her profit from the trade was twice as much as she had expected.

Marriage proposal: Khadījah was already a widow. She did not plan to marry again. Now after the trade from Syria, her admiration for Muhammad (S) increased. She was impressed to see the honesty and integrity of Muhammad (S). She thought that if she were to marry again, she would marry a person who was good in character and who was trustworthy. She realized Muhammad (S) was that person. She sent a marriage proposal to him.

Muhammad (S) was 25 years old at that time. He was not married yet. When Muhammad (S) received the marriage proposal, he agreed to it. He knew Khadījah was 15 years older than him, but it did not matter. He thought Khadījah would be a good woman to marry because she was honest, kind hearted, generous and above all she was a noble lady among the Quraish. They got married in the year 595 C.E.

First 15 years of marriage: During the first fifteen years of marriage, the Prophet (S) and Khadījah had six children born to them—two sons and four daughters. Both the sons died during their infancy or early childhood.

Life after revelation: After Muhammad (S) received the revelation from Allāh, Khadījah accepted Islam and became the first Muslimah. She spent her wealth for the cause of Islam. She did everything to help her husband spread the message of Islam. She supported him during good and bad times. When people mistreated the Prophet (S), she would comfort and console him. Both the Prophet (S) and Khadījah had many difficulties in their lives. The people in Makkah did not like them because Muhammad (S) was preaching Islam.

In order to stop the Prophet (S) from preaching Islam, the Quraish boycotted the Muslims for three years. To boycott means to dump and cut off all relationship. During this time all the Muslims had to go outside of Makkah and live there without any contact with the Makkan people. At that time Khadījah suffered enormous strain, but she never complained. She continued to support the Muslims and the Prophet (S). She showed extraordinary patience and perseverance.

Death of Khadījah: After the three year period was over, the Muslims returned to Makkah. Khadījah became weak due to the long suffering from the boycott. She passed away in 620 C.E. at the age of 65. It was a great loss for the Prophet (S). He missed her and often remembered her with respect. All Muslims have many good things to learn from her life.

from**hadith**

It is narrated that when Khadījah had passed away, Muhammad (S) had said: "She believed in me when no one else did. She accepted Islam when people disbelieved in Islam. She helped me and comforted me when there was no helper."

1. How old was Khadījah and Muhammad (S) when they got married?

    (a)   She was 25, he was 40
    (b)   She was 40, he was 25
    (c)   She was 30, he was 65
    (d)   She was 30, he was 25

2. How long was the Prophet (S) married to Khadījah?

    (a)   15 years
    (b)   20 years
    (c)   25 years
    (d)   40 years

3. After Muhammad (S) received revelation, how long did Khadījah live?

    _____

4. A servant of Khadījah's observed Muhammad (S) in Syria about the way he conducted the business. What was the name of this servant?

    _____

5. Khadījah supported Muhammad (S) in many different ways. Write any three ways she supported him.

    (a)   _____

    (b)   _____

    (c)   _____

6.   Find words: KHADIJAH, ABYSSINIA, MAKKAH, SYRIA, ISLAM, MUSLIM, QURAISH, KUBRA, BOYCOTT, SUFFERING, WEALTH,

A	R	T	B	O	Y	C	O	T	T
K	H	A	D	I	J	A	H	M	X
W	D	G	U	S	Q	B	N	T	E
E	U	K	G	L	S	Y	R	I	A
A	Q	U	R	A	I	S	H	W	H
L	B	B	B	M	U	S	L	I	M
T	A	R	W	U	C	I	P	J	F
H	P	A	T	I	E	N	C	E	L
S	U	F	F	E	R	I	N	G	O
A	R	M	A	K	K	A	H	K	E

'Ā'ishah (ra): *Beloved Wife of the Prophet (S)*

Objective of the Lesson:

'Ā'ishah (ra) was the most beloved wife of the Prophet (S). The students will learn about this great woman—her personality and her life as the wife of the Prophet (S). Students will also learn an incident about her lost necklace and its implication upon the Muslim community.

For most of his life, Prophet Muhammad (S) had one wife. At one stage in his life he had to marry many women for many different reasons. This stage was between his age of 55 and 60 years. During this stage he married a woman by the name of 'Ā'ishah (ra). She was his most beloved wife.

'Ā'ishah's (ra) father was Abū Bakr and mother was Umm Rumman. The date of her birth is not known. Muslim scholars mentioned different years as her birth year. Some scholars say she was probably born in 613 C.E. but many others say she was born several years earlier.

Childhood: 'Ā'ishah accepted Islam as a child when her father became a Muslim. In the early years of Islam the Quraish were against Islam. They used to torture the Muslims. To avoid the torture many Muslims migrated to Ethiopia. 'Ā'ishah and her father also migrated to Ethiopia. After a few years they returned to Makkah. Then in 622 C.E. the Prophet (S) migrated to Madīnah to avoid enemies in Makkah. During the migration, her father Abū Bakr was with the Prophet (S). Soon 'Ā'ishah and her elder sister 'Asma also migrated to Madīnah.

Marriage of 'Ā'ishah: When 'Ā'ishah migrated to Madīnah, her father got her married to the Prophet (S). Islamic thinkers do not agree about the age when 'Ā'ishah got married. Some Hadīth say she was engaged with the

Khadijah
Sawda   Hasfsa
Umm Habiba   Zainab bint Jahsh

Wives of Muhammad (S)

'Ā'ishah

Zainab II   Safiyyah
Maymunah   Juwairiyah
Rehana   Umm Salama
Mariah

Prophet (S) when she was six years old and actually got married when she was nine years old. Some other Hadīth indicate she was between twelve and nineteen years old when she got married.

It was normal at that time for girls to get married at young age. Today life has changed; boys and girls do not get married at an early age. However, about a hundred years ago in the USA it was normal for girls to get married early. In many countries it was common for girls to get married at very young age. At the time of the Prophet (S) it was normal for girls to get married at an early age. There was nothing wrong or unusual about early marriages.

Beloved wife: 'Ā'ishah was very intelligent and wise for her young age. As a wife of the Prophet (S), she took care of the needs of the Prophet (S) and gave him support during the difficult times of Islam. During the Battle of Uhud, she not only nursed her wounded husband, but she also took care of other injured Muslims. She also carried water for the Muslims who were in the battleground. The Prophet (S) loved her very much. They did not have any children born to them. At the time when the Prophet (S) passed away, he put his head on the lap of 'Ā'ishah and breathed his last.

'Ā'ishah and her necklace: Once 'Ā'ishah was traveling with Muhammad (S) in a large caravan. The caravan rested for the night at one place. Next 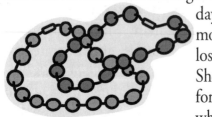 day early in the morning 'Ā'ishah lost her necklace. She was searching for the necklace when the caravan left without realizing 'Ā'ishah was still searching. Much later the caravan realized 'Ā'ishah was not in the caravan and they had lost her. Nobody was sure when she was lost. Next morning she was rejoined with the caravan. At that time some bad people spread rumor about her saying that she

purposely stayed back. The Prophet (S) was very upset since people were talking bad things about her. Allāh sent a revelation asking people not to follow Shaitān. Allāh condemned those who accuse the believing women. The Qur'an says that people who accuse the honest women would suffer serious punishment.[24:23] 'Ā'ishah was innocent.

Life after the Prophet (S): After the Prophet (S) passed away, none of his wives were allowed to marry other men.[33:53] This was because these women were honored as "**mother of believers.**" The Qur'ān prohibited any men from marrying them. 'Ā'ishah mostly lived in Madīnah, but time to time she went to Makkah to do Hajj. She spent most of her life to educate Muslim women about Islam. She narrated several Hadīth that she learned by watching the Prophet (S). People consider her Hadīth to be very reliable.

As a teacher: 'Ā'ishah was an extraordinary teacher. She had great depth of knowledge about the Qur'ān, Hadīth, fiqh, medicine and history. On several occasions, she had corrected others on religious issues. It is estimated that she had about 200 students; some of them were prominent sahābah.

Battle of the Camels: Several years later, khalīfa 'Uthman was killed by some people. These people wanted 'Ali to become the next khalīfa. When 'Ali became the khalīfa, he was investigating the murder of 'Uthman. 'Ā'ishah thought 'Ali would not punish the killers. To ensure that justice was served, she led an army against 'Ali. The army of 'Ali and 'Ā'ishah fought a battle. Muslims were killing Muslims in the battle. It was a sad situation. 'Ā'ishah was riding a camel and was directing the battle like a true army general. For this reason the battle was later known as the **Battle of the Camels**. In the battle 'Ā'ishah's army was defeated. She was captured by 'Ali. He sent her back to Madīnah under military protection.

She lived in Madīnah for the rest of her life. It is

reported that she passed away in the year 678 C.E., i.e. in 56 A.H. There was space available near the resting places of prophet Muhammad (S) and Abū Bakr (r). She did not want her resting place to be superior to other wives of the prophet who already died. Therefore, she was buried in *Jannatul Baqi*.

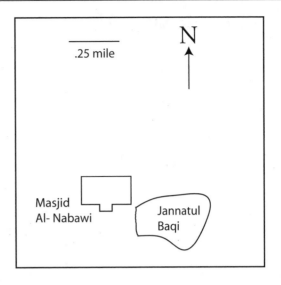

Interesting Facts:

Jannatul Baqi, in Madīnah, is the graveyard of many of the companions, including the martyrs of the Battle of Uhud.

All the wives of the Prophet (S), except Khadījah, were buried in this honored place.

The grave (rowdha) of our dear Rasulullah (S) is inside the complex of Masjid al-Nabawi. The graves of Abū Bakr and 'Umar are next to the rowdha (burial ground) of Rasulullah (S).

1. Those who want to bring charge against good and noble women, they are required to bring certain number of witnesses. How many witnesses are needed? Read the verse 24:4 to answer.

_____

2. If the required number of witnesses is not produced, then charge against woman cannot be established. What does Allāh say about those who cannot bring the witness yet blame the woman? Read verse 24:13 to answer.

_____

3. The famous Battle of the Camels was fought between two important people in history. Who were they?

    (a)   'Ā'ishah and Abū Bakr
    (b)   'Ā'ishah and 'Ali
    (c)   'Ā'ishah and 'Uthman
    (d)   'Uthman and 'Ali

4. Those who accuse chaste and believing woman are condemned and they will face punishment in the Hereafter. Testimony against them will be brought. Read sūrah An-Nūr verses 23 and 24 to answer what will bear testimony against them.

    (a) _____ (b) _____ (c) _____

5. How many children were born to 'Ā'ishah and Prophet Muhammad (S)?

    (a)   One child.
    (b)   Two children.
    (c)   Five children.
    (d)   No children were born to them.

6. What happened when 'Ā'ishah went to search for the lost necklace?

    (a)   Her caravan was attacked.
    (b)   The caravan left without her.
    (c)   The caravan came back to pick her up.
    (d)   The caravan waited for one full day.

Fātimah (ra): *The Lady of The Light*

Objective of the Lesson:

Fātimah (ra) was the youngest and most beloved daughter of the Prophet (S). She was the wife of 'Ali (R), the fourth Khalīfa. The students will study her life and her sacrifices to understand the greatness of this woman.

In this lesson we will learn about the Prophet's daughter Fātimah bint Muhammad (ra). We will study the history from the Sunni point of view. The Sunnis are those Muslims who follow the sunnah or the doings of the Prophet (S). Among the Muslims there is another group called Shī'ah who follow 'Ali as their Imam. In the world about 80% of the Muslims are Sunnis and about 15% are Shī'ah and the rest are other types of Muslims. We will learn about Shī'ah in 8th and 9th grade in detail.

The Sunni account of Fātimah is slightly different from the Shī'ah account.

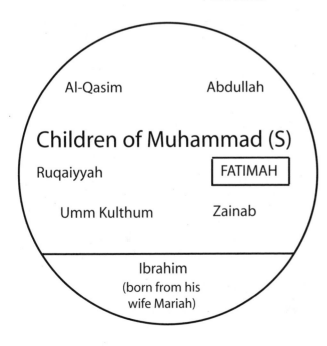

Al-Qasim   Abdullah

Children of Muhammad (S)

Ruqaiyyah   FATIMAH

Umm Kulthum   Zainab

Ibrahim
(born from his
wife Mariah)

Prophet's daughter: Fātimah was the fifth child of Muhammad (S) and Khadījah. Fātimah had three elder sisters and one elder brother. The brother died during childhood. Her sisters were Ruqaiyah, Umm Kulthum and Zainab. Fātimah's full name was Fātimah bint Muhammad. But during her later life she was also known as **Fātimah az-Zahrā**. Az-Zahrā means the Lady of the Light. She was born in the year 605 C.E.—five years before Muhammad (S) received prophethood. The Prophet (S) was 35 years old at that time. She lived for only 28 or 29 years and passed away a few months after the Prophet (S) left the world .

Fātimah's childhood: During childhood Fātimah found friends and playmates among her sisters. Her brother Qasim died before she was born. There were

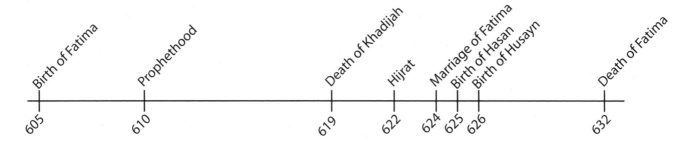

Birth of Fatima — 605
Prophethood — 610
Death of Khadijah — 619
Hijrat — 622
Marriage of Fatima — 624
Birth of Hasan — 625
Birth of Husayn — 626
Death of Fatima — 632

other members in her father's house, including 'Ali and Zaid inb Harith.

When Fātimah was five years old, one day she heard that her father became the prophet of Allāh, which means he received God's message. Her mother explained to her what it meant and how much responsibility her father had to take as rasulullāh. Since then she became more closely attached to her father and began taking care of him with deep affection. She would follow her father wherever she could and pay attention to whatever he said.

Girl of strong mind: Since her early childhood Fātimah grew up with strong determination and personality. By watching her father, she learned to stand up against injustice. She also showed supreme patience, a quality she inherited from her parents.

One day when she was only ten years old, she accompanied her father to Masjid al-Haram where the Ka'bah is located. Her father went there to pray. There were a few people who did not like her father and did not like his teachings. When her father was praying, these people continued to taunt him. Then one person collected rotten intestines of a slaughtered animal and poured it over her father when he was doing sujud. This enraged Fātimah. She ran to her father and began to remove the smelly, filthy substance from her father's body. Then she stood up and shouted back at the people for their dirty work.

On another occasion, when she and her father were doing tawaf around the Ka'bah, some bad people wanted to strangle her father. She screamed and shouted for help. At that point Abū Bakr rushed to the scene and rescued the Prophet (S).

When a bad neighbor poured dust on the head of the Prophet (S), Fātimah cried and wiped off the dust from her father's head.

Influence of her mother: During Fātimah's childhood, her loving mother Khadījah deeply influenced her. She learned many values from her mother. She noticed how much Khadījah used to take care of Muhammad (S) during good times and bad times. From her she also learned the qualities to take care of her father. The Quraish once boycotted the Prophet (S) and his family for three long years. It was a difficult time for everybody in the family. During this time she helped her mother to prepare food or fetch water from distant places.

After the boycott was withdrawn, her mother Khadījah became weak and she passed away in the year 619 C.E. After the death of her mother, Fātimah took the responsibility of taking care of her father.

Influence of the sisters: Fātimah's amazing personality was developed from her early childhood. Experiences gained during early childhood shaped her personality. She was much saddened when two of her sisters were divorced. Their husbands were against the Prophet (S). She became stronger by noticing how much people disliked the truth and how much they wanted to stop the truth.

Influence of her father: Fātimah received the strongest influence from her father, Muhammad

(S). She learned from him the quality of leadership. During the battles, she would feed the troops and dress her father's wounds. Whenever necessary she led the prayers for the women and discussed religious matters with them. She had the special skill of speaking, a quality learned from her father. She was kind and gentle, like her father. She was very affectionate and kind to the poor. She would often give them all the food she had at home.

The Prophet (S) loved her very much. He once said: "Fātimah is a part of me and whoever makes her angry makes me angry." Her devotion to her father earned her the loving nickname "**umm abi-ha**" which means "**mother of her father**".

Fātimah's family: Fātimah was married to 'Ali in the year 624 C.E., about two years after hijrat to Madīnah. One year later, she was blessed with a boy. They named him Hasan. Within a year she was blessed with another son. They named him Husayn. She also had a daughter born to her. She

named her Zainab, after her sister. She used to bring her children to the Prophet (S) and he loved to play with them. Even after her marriage, she and her husband remained close to the Prophet (S).

Last days of the Prophet (S): Fātimah accompanied the Prophet (S) in umrah after the Treaty of Hudaibiyah. She accompanied the Muslims when Makkah was liberated.

After the Farewell Pilgrimage, the Prophet (S) told Fātimah that angel Jibril used to recite the Qur'ān once every year with him, but in that year he recited it with the Prophet (S) twice. This meant he would not live too long. When the Prophet (S) fell sick after the **Farewell Pilgrimage**, Fātimah continued to visit him. One day the Prophet (S) whispered something in her ear and she started to cry. Then he said something again, and she started to smile. When the Prophet's wife enquired what happened, she told her that first he said he would die very soon. At this she started crying. Then he said she would be the first person to join him in the after-life. At this she smiled. Within about six months after the Prophet (S) passed away, Fātimah also passed away.

The Prophet's dearest daughter: Except Fātimah, all of the Prophet's children died before the Prophet (S) passed away. This means her sisters died before her. Her brothers died during childhood or infancy. She survived her father.

In Fātimah, the Prophet (S) found a daughter, a friend and a close companion throughout his life as a prophet. All Muslims have great regard for her. She was a good example of piety. Women at that time used to respect her very much.

She had a very unique distinction in the history of Islam. First of all, she was the daughter of the Prophet (S). Second, she was the wife of 'Ali, who was the fourth khalīfa. 'Ali was regarded as the first Imam of the Shī'ah. Therefore, she was also the wife of the first Shī'ah Imam. Her two sons were the second and third Imams of the Shī'ah. From her descendants, at one point, the famous Fātimid Dynasty was established.

homework**weekend 18**

1. Write the names of the children of the Prophet (S) born to him form his wife Khadījah (ra).

2. In which year according to the Sunni viewpoint Fātimah was born?

    (a) 595 C.E.
    (b) 600 C.E.
    (c) 605 C.E.
    (d) 610 C.E.

3. How long did Fātimah live?

    (a) About 20 years
    (b) About 28 years
    (c) About 38 years
    (d) About 40 years

4. Write two of the loving nicknames by which Fātimah was known.

    (a) ______________________________

    (b) ______________________________

5. When the Prophet was in death bed, why did Fātimah first cry and then smile? Write in your own words.

____

____

____

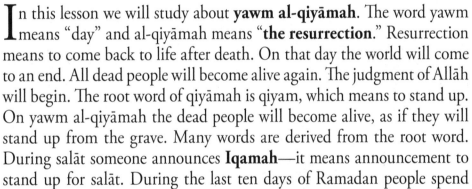

Al-Qiyāmah: *The Awakening*

Objective of the Lesson:

All Muslims are required to have firm belief in the Awakening. The Qur'ān has described the Awakening in many different ways. Students will study the Qur'ānic descriptions of the Awakening and understand the purpose of the Awakening and why it is important for all Muslims to believe in its happening.

In this lesson we will study about **yawm al-qiyāmah**. The word yawm means "day" and al-qiyāmah means "**the resurrection.**" Resurrection means to come back to life after death. On that day the world will come to an end. All dead people will become alive again. The judgment of Allāh will begin. The root word of qiyāmah is qiyam, which means to stand up. On yawm al-qiyāmah the dead people will become alive, as if they will stand up from the grave. Many words are derived from the root word. During salāt someone announces **Iqamah**—it means announcement to stand up for salāt. During the last ten days of Ramadan people spend day and night in mosque to pray to Allāh. It is called **qiyamul layl** or the night of standing up.

Yawm al-qiyāmah is known by many other names in English. The Resurrection is the main name. It is also known as **the Awakening, the Hour, the Day of Account, the Day of Gathering, the Day of Distress, the Day of Calculation**. Each name indicates one special thing about the Day.

Belief in yawm al-qiyāmah: The yawm al-qiyāmah will happen in the future. Only Allāh knows when it will happen. We do not know the date and time of the day. As a Muslim we must believe that yawm al-qiyāmah will happen. Belief in yawm al-qiyāmah is part of our 'Iman or faith. The Qur'ān has talked about yawm al-qiyāmah in many sūrahs and many verses. Sūrah 75 is named al-qiyāmah, where it describes various things that will happen on that Day. Even with these description, we cannot fully understand the Qiyāmah. We can only attempt to understand it based on how the Qur'ān and Hadīth of the Prophet (S) described it.

How it will begin: Qiyāmah will happen all of a sudden, when people are not at all prepared for it. When Allāh will decide it to happen, He will tell angel **Israfil** to blow a trumpet. After the trumpet is blown, al-qiyāmah will begin.[6:74; 18:99; 20]

What will happen: At the time of qiyāmah a number of things will happen. The earth will be destroyed on the day of qiyāmah.[56:4; 69:14; 89:21] The earth will give out her contents on that day.[84:4; 99:1-5] Everything will collapse and all the human beings will faint.[39:68] The sky will rent apart.[55:37; 69:16] The mountains will crumble and some mountains will vaporize away like clouds. People will want to get relief from the day, but nobody will get any relief. Faces of sinners will be sad. Eyes of people will be awe struck and they will stare in horror. The

nursing mothers will forget their babies, mankind will be like drunken people but they will not be drunk.

What else will happen: On that Day, nothing will appear to work in their normal ways. Mankind will be like moths scattered around.[101:4] The earth will be changed into another earth.[14:48] The earth will be leveled plain. Wild beast will be gathered

together. The sun and the stars will lose their lights. Seas will become like blazing fire. Pregnant women will drop their babies from their bodies.[22:2] Hell will be brought near.[89:23] No friend will ask for a friend.[70:10] No person will have power to do

anything for another person.[82:19] In spite of such a chaos, the believers will be under the shade and with springs and fruits.[77:41-43] Paradise will be brought near.[81:13] Countless other things will happen on that Day.

Why al-qiyāmah: The main purpose of al-qiyāmah is to bring justice. Sometimes we see that bad people keep on doing bad things and they do not get punished. We also see that good people keep on doing good things but they do not get rewards or their suffering does not end. We should remember, bad people will not escape punishment in the long run and good people will ultimately get their rewards. The purpose of al-qiyāmah is to deliver justice and Allāh's justice is accurate and very fair. Those who do a tiny amount of good work will get reward for it and those who do a tiny amount of sin will get punishment for it. Nobody can escape from the judgment of Allāh. Al-qiyāmah is the day when Allāh will decide who will go to Heaven and who will suffer severe punishment in the Fire.

What about the deeds of the people: On that Day everybody will receive his or her dues in full.[3:185] Written pages of our deeds will be laid open in front of everybody.[81:11] Everybody will be confronted with all the good and bad deeds they have done in the earth. Each person will clearly know what he or she has left behind—i.e. the things they were required to do but did not do, e.g. salāt or paying zakāt. Whoever has done good or evil equal to the weight of an atom will see it.[100:7-8] It will be a hard

day for the people who do not believe. Everybody will be given their records in their hands. The righteous people will receive it in their right hand, but the sinners will get it in their left hand.[84:7-15] The sinners will bite their hands in regret.[25:27]

What can we do now: The Day of Qiyāmah is certain to happen. Nobody can escape it. However, we can prepare ourselves to face the Day of Qiyāmah. People who live a good life on earth will have no fear on the Day of Qiyāmah. The righteous people will be rewarded on the Day of Judgment. Only the sinners are going to be punished. Therefore we should prepare ourselves by doing good works always. We should do our salāt on time, pray to Allāh, fast in the month of Ramadan, give charity and do all types of good work that Allāh likes. If we continue to be good people, on the Day of Qiyāmah we will have no fear—we will be successful in the Hereafter.

Answer what would happen on the Day of Resurrection as mentioned in the following verses:

1. In verse 25:27: What would sinners do? _____

2. In verse 69:19: What will be given to the righteous? _____

_____

3. In verse 82:5: What would a person know? _____

_____

4. In verse 52:9: What would happen to the heaven? _____

_____

5. In verse 18:47: What would happen to the mountain? _____

_____

6. In verse 20:124: What would happen to the sinners? _____

_____

Rūh and Nafs: *An Overview*

Objective of the Lesson:

Rūh and Nafs are two states of human existence. Both are used to describe the soul of human being. But there are differences. This lesson discusses the differences between both the terms in a simple language.

Farhad, Nahid and Bilal were lucky; each of them received gifts of more than five hundred dollars when they graduated from elementary school to middle school. None of them ever had such a large amount of money. Earlier Farhad only had a maximum of fifty-five dollars, which he spent on four books. Nahid had saved little over a hundred dollars over the last few years. Bilal never had more than twenty dollars as he always bought CDs and games every time he had some money.

Today was different. Each had more than five hundred dollars. They counted twice, and then once again. It was truly more than five hundred! Farhad thought he should spend some money on books and some on his soccer training fees. Nahid planned to give some money to local masjid, and some to the charity for the earthquake victims. She would save some money for her college. Bilal never had any problem deciding how to spend this money. He always knew he wanted new game system, and six more games. Wireless control and a new sound system are still beyond this amount.

Each had more than five hundred dollars and each had so many different plans.

Let us relate the above to our life to understand rūh and nafs. Everyone has the gift of life. Some live for a few years more, some less. Yet we all spend our lives in so many different ways.

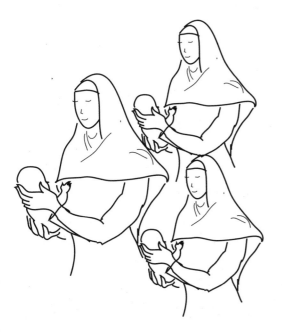

What can a life do? When Allāh (swt) creates human beings, He infuses them with His *Rūh*. The *Rūh* is considered the spirit of a person. A baby in a mother's womb is living, yet incomplete. The baby becomes a complete individual[15:29] when Allāh (swt) breathes His *Rūh* into the baby. With this *Rūh*, the baby is no more a mix of muscles, bones and skin. It is now an individual. When the baby grows up, he or she will be spending the life in any way possible.

We know little about the *Rūh*.[17:85] In the Qur'ān Allāh has used two terms to describe the spirit or soul—one is the *Rūh*, while the other term is the *Nafs*.

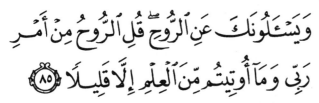

And they ask you as to the Rūh. You say: "The Rūh is at the command of my Rabb, and you have not been given of the knowledge except a little." (Bani Isra'il 17:85)

The *Rūh* is the gift of spirit from Allāh (swt), while the *Nafs* is how we handle the spirit. *Rūh* is the finest form of spirit, without any error or evil. The Qur'ān never used the word *Rūh* to describe any evil. We may consider the *Rūh* to be a supply for leading our life. Allāh (swt) gives this supply in equal amount to all the people. Some people use the supply carefully, while others waste it.

Farhad, Nahid and Bilal each used their five hundred dollars in different ways. Probably they

would use their spirit in different ways too. When the supply—the spirit is in the possession of a person, we may consider it to be the *Nafs*.

'Isā (A) is specifically mentioned to have received the *Rūh*. 'Isā (A) is thus known as *Rūh-ullah* or a Spirit of Allāh (swt). This shows that the birth of 'Isā (A) was not evil. Receiving the *Rūh* is an honor not specific to 'Isā (A) only. Allāh (swt) gives his *Rūh* to all Muslims,[58:22] even to all the people.[15:29] The *Rūh* provides us the strength and guidance to remain in the right path.[58:22] In contrast, the *Nafs* is prone to evil.[12:53]

Rūh can be angels: The Qur'ān has used the term *Rūh* to describe angles as well. Jibril (A) has been named *Rūh-ul-Quddus* or the Holy

Spirit. Allāh (swt) has also mentioned Jibril (A) to be the *Rūh al-Amin*, or the Faithful Spirit.[26:193] The Qur'ān itself is also called the *Rūh*—the inspiration or the Spirit of the Mankind.[17:85]

The first few verses of the Qur'ān were revealed on *Lailatul Qadr* or the Night of Majesty. In this night, the angles and the *Rūh* descend on mankind with all the Decrees and peace.[97:4-5]

Three stages of Nafs: We already mentioned the *Nafs* is the soul which is not the same as the *Rūh*. While the *Rūh* is the divine form of spirit and requires no improvement, the *Nafs* passes through three stages to reach perfection.

Early stage of the Nafs: The first stage for the Nafs is *Ammarah*, which is the animal stage.[12:53] In this stage the action of a person is not appropriate for a normal human being. The person is prone to evil and is ruled by emotions. He cannot control temptations. He makes bad decisions. He does evil. To him, good deeds do not make much sense. Bad deeds are much more enjoyable for him.

Middle stage of the Nafs: If the person continues to improve, s/he reaches a stage of *Lawwamah*, which is the self-critical human stage.[75:2] In this stage, the person reviews his or her actions and continues to improve. The person rejects bad deeds, and works on good deeds. He or she has to think before doing the good deed. Good acts do not come easily to him or her. The actions of a person in this stage are better than the animal stage, yet there is a scope for further improvement.

Final stage of the Nafs: The final stage, which should be the goal of all the people, is *Mutma'innah* or Heavenly stage.[89:27] In this final stage, a person has total control over himself, and does not struggle to avoid bad acts. Good deeds come automatically to these people. They would not do any bad deed, even if the bad deed seems enjoyable. People who achieve this stage return to Allāh (swt) with pleasure and happiness. People from this stage are welcomed to the Garden of Allāh (swt).[89:30]

بِسْمِ اللهِ الرَّحْمٰنِ الرَّحِيمِ

إِنَّا أَنزَلْنَٰهُ فِى لَيْلَةِ ٱلْقَدْرِ ۝ وَمَآ أَدْرَىٰكَ مَا لَيْلَةُ ٱلْقَدْرِ ۝ لَيْلَةُ ٱلْقَدْرِ خَيْرٌ مِّنْ أَلْفِ شَهْرٍ ۝ تَنَزَّلُ ٱلْمَلَٰٓئِكَةُ وَٱلرُّوحُ فِيهَا بِإِذْنِ رَبِّهِم مِّن كُلِّ أَمْرٍ ۝ سَلَٰمٌ هِىَ حَتَّىٰ مَطْلَعِ ٱلْفَجْرِ ۝

Al-Qadr
(Revealed at Makkah)
With the name of Allāh, most Gracious, most Rewarding.

1 Surely We have revealed it during the Night of Majesty.
2 And what will make you comprehend what the Night of Majesty is?
3 The Night of Majesty is better than a thousand months.
4 The angels and the Ruh descend in it by the permission of their Rabb concerning every affair.
5 Salam. It is till the rising of the dawn.

1. Read Sūrah Az-Zumar, verse 42. What are the two times that Allāh (swt) takes away the Nafs from the people?

   a. _____

   b. _____

2. Read verse 40:15. What kind of Rūh is mentioned in this verse?

   _____

3. Read Sūrah Bani Isra'il, verse 85, and then answer the following:

   a. Who commands the Spirit? _____

   b. How much do we know about the Spirit? _____

4. How does Allāh (swt) infuse the Rūh in human? Find the answer in Sūrah Sād, verses 72.

   _____

5. Read Sūrah Yūsuf, verse 53. Every soul is prone to evil, except whom?

   _____

6. In verse 89:28, Allāh (swt) tells how He invites the people who reach the final state of the soul, the *Nafsul-Mutma'innah*. What is this invitation?

   _____

7. Name the three stages through which Nafs passes.

   (a) _____

   (b) _____

   (c) _____

The Angels and The Jinn: *An Overview*

Objective of the Lesson:

The angels and the jinn are invisible beings, created by Allāh. Their roles and the goals of life are different. The students will study about the main differences between the two entities and understand what are their specific duties or activities.

The angels and the jinn are among the many creations of Allāh. In Arabic, the angels are called malaks. Although we cannot see the angels, they are everywhere. They support the **arsh** or the Seat of Power of Allāh.[40:7] This means that they carry out the orders of Allāh. Malaks cannot disobey the orders of Allāh.[66:6] They cannot choose between right and wrong. They always glorify Allāh.[40:7] To believe in the existence of the malaks is a part of our faith.[2:177]

Names of angels: The Qur'ān and the Hadīth names some of the malaks. Angel Jibril brought the messages of the Qur'ān to Muhammad (S). Angel Mikal[2:98] is provides nourishment to the body and the soul. Angel Israfil is responsible to blow the trumpet at the time of the Awakening. Angel Azrail is responsible for collecting the souls of people when they die. People of Babylon were used to sorcery. Angels Hārūt and Mārūt came to them and told the people to believe in Allāh.[2:102] Angel Malik is the in-charge of Hell.[43:77]

Roles in battles: In difficult times, malaks help the righteous people. During the Battle of Badr, Rasulullah (S) had only 313 soldiers, while the enemies had 1000 soldiers. Allāh had sent one thousand malaks to assist Rasulallah (S) during this battle.[8:9]

During the Battle of Uhud, three thousand angels assisted the Muslims.[3:124] With this Divine help, Muslims were able to defeat a stronger enemy.

Position of angels: Malaks are not superior to man. When Allāh created Adam, angels expressed doubt about the nature of man. Once Adam was created and given the intellect, all the angels submitted to him.[2:34] When the Qur'ān was being revealed to the Prophet (S) many ignorant people believed angels were daughters of Allāh.

Main job: The main job of the angels is to worship and praise Allāh. Their other job is to bring messages. They bring messages of rewards if we do good deeds.[41:30-31] They also pray for us for our forgiveness.[40:7-9] Angels are friends of Muslims, both in this world as well as in the Hereafter.[41:31] Since angels are everywhere, they watch us from all sides and protect us.[13:11] They also record our good and bad deeds.[43:80, 82:10-12]

When people die, Malak of death comes to collect the soul.[32:11] When a good person dies the angels greet him or her with salām.[16:32] However, they are stern when an evil person dies.

Jinn: The jinn are created out of scorching fire.[15:27] The word jinn suggests some creature that is

concealed or remains hidden. Some jinn are evil, while other jinn are righteous. Both humans and jinn are created to worship Allāh.[51:56]

وَمَا خَلَقْتُ ٱلْجِنَّ وَٱلْإِنسَ إِلَّا لِيَعْبُدُونِ ۝

And I have not created the jinn and the mankind but that they should worship me. (51:56)

Just as some people refuse to worship Allāh, there are also jinn who refuse to obey Allāh.

More about the jinn: We should not confuse jinn as demons. Rather, they are creatures who are hidden from common sight. Would you be surprised to know that jinn also had rasuls among them?[6:131] It is, thus, possible that they are a special kind of people who keep themselves away from the common people. This separation with common people happens as jinn have advanced power or abilities. The word "genius" comes from the word jinn.

Jinn listened to the Qur'ān: Some jinn attentively listened to the Qur'ān and became Muslims.[46:29] They then went back to their own communities and preached Islam.[46:30] They realized that the Qur'ān brought the truth just as long back similar truth was sent to Mūsā (A). Some scholars says this group of jinn was most likely the intelligent Jewish leaders, because their interest was in Mūsā (A).

Another group of jinn were also very impressed with the Qur'ān.[72:1] According to some descriptions, these jinn were seven in number. It is reported that these jinn came from a town called Nasibain, which is in current day Iraq. These jinn realized that Allāh never had a spouse, nor did He have a child.[72:3] They also understood that such allegations against Allāh were absolute lies.[72:4] Some scholars say that this group of jinn were most likely the Christian scholars, because their interest was about the position of 'Isā (A) in Islam.

While some jinn were rasuls and some became Muslims, other jinn were evil. Iblīs, the Shaitān, was from the jinn.[18:50] Since many jinn are smooth talkers,[6:113] Allāh has advised us to protect ourselves from the evil suggestions of jinn and man alike.[114:6] Jinn and man sometimes may work together, but their combined effort cannot make anything similar to the Qur'ān.[17:88] Sulaimān (A) had employed jinn to work for him.[34:12] Some people say that such jinn were most likely the people of extraordinary abilities.

Evil ideas from the jinn: Although some jinn listened to the Qur'an, and there were rasuls amongst the jinn, they also give us evil ideas. One such jinn is Iblīs, who is a sworn enemy of the mankind. In sūrah an-Nās, we pray to Allāh to protect us from the evil prompting from the jinn and the man.

بِسْمِ اللَّهِ الرَّحْمَٰنِ الرَّحِيمِ

قُلْ أَعُوذُ بِرَبِّ النَّاسِ ۝ مَلِكِ النَّاسِ ۝ إِلَٰهِ النَّاسِ ۝ مِن شَرِّ الْوَسْوَاسِ الْخَنَّاسِ ۝ الَّذِى يُوَسْوِسُ فِي صُدُورِ النَّاسِ ۝ مِنَ الْجِنَّةِ وَالنَّاسِ ۝

Surah An-Nas
(Revealed at Makkah)
With the name of Allāh, most Gracious, most Rewarding
1 SAY: "I take refuge with the Rabb of mankind,
2 "the Master of mankind,
3 "the God of mankind,
4 "from the evil of the whisperings of the sneaking one,—
5 "who whispers into the hearts of mankind,
6 "from among the jinn or the mankind."

homework**weekend 21**

1. Read sūrah As-Shūra, verse 42:5. What do the angels do for those in the earth?

    _____

    _____

2. Read sūrah Al-Baqarah, verse 30, and then answer the following:

    a. What did Allāh (swt) tell the angels? _____

    _____

    b. What did the angels say? _____

    _____

    _____.

3. From sūrah 66, verse 6, write four qualities of the angels who guard the Hellfire:

    1. _____ 2. _____ 3. _____

    _____ 4. _____

4. There is a sūrah in the Qur'ān which is named after either the malaks or the jinns. Which sūrah is that?

    _____

5. Copy the translation sūrah Bani Isrā'īl, verse 88 in the space below:

    _____

    _____

    _____

    _____

Shaitān: *The Invisible Enemy*

Objective of the Lesson:

Shatiān's strategy is to divert the people from worshipping Allāh and ultimately destroy them. Shaitān is not a scary monster, but he talks sweetly to raise false desire in our mind. The lesson shows some of the strategies of Shaitān. The students will learn how to identify the temptations of Shaitān and how to avoid the whispering of the evil.

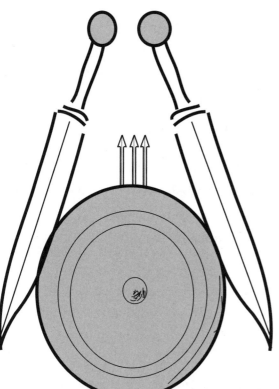

Of all the things that Allāh (swt) created, creation of Shaitān is most puzzling. We may ask, why did Allāh (swt) create something that tells us to do bad things? Without Shaitān, we would not be doing bad acts, and we would not be sinners. So why does Shaitān exist?

Shaitān is a test for us: The role of Shaitān is to provide us many bad options in life and make us believe the bad options as the best choice for us. Shaitān is a test for us as we lead our lives. In our school exam we have multiple choice questions. One choice is correct and the rest are wrong. If we do not take the exam, we cannot progress to the next level in our school or in our sports. Our life is like an exam. In order to progress spiritually, we need tests in the form of temptations by Shaitān.[4:119] Allāh (swt) gave Shaitān the permission to test people until the Day of Judgment.[7:14-15] In this exam Shaitān provides too many choices that seem correct. He will whisper in your heart and tell you which choice to select. He always tells us to select the wrong choice.

Angels do not require any testing. Since human beings are superior to angels, they need testing and they progress to higher levels after qualifying in the tests.

Our enemy: Shaitān is the main enemy of mankind. In the Qur'ān Allāh (swt) says:

إِنَّ ٱلشَّيْطَـٰنَ لِلْإِنسَـٰنِ عَدُوٌّ مُّبِينٌ ۝

...Surely Shaitān is an open enemy to mankind. (12:5)

He wants to prove that he has the ability to mislead human beings. If he can mislead people, he thinks he can claim to be better than human beings.

Invisible to us: Unlike the popular picture of Satan being a scary demon, who has long horns and pointy teeth, Shaitān is invisible to us.[7:27] Shaitān can see us, while we cannot see his true nature.

Temptation of Shaitān: He makes bad things tempting to us.[16:63]

...Shaitān made fair-seeming to them their deeds, so that he is their patron today, and for them is a painful punishment. (16:63)

He encourages us to do bad things.[4:119] He does not scare us by thunderous voice, but whispers into our hearts.[114:5] He tells people that he is their best friend.[7:21]

"Most certainly I am to you of the sincere advisers." (7:21)

He fools them into the darkness of bad actions.[2:257] Once men are in trouble, he quickly leaves them to suffer in their trouble.[14:22] He does not even take any blame for the troubles that men are facing.[14:22]

...Shaitān will say: "Surely Allah promised you the promise of truth; I promised you, but I broke to you. And I had no any authority over you, except that I called you and you responded to me; therefore do not blame me, but blame yourselves. I cannot be your rescuer, nor can you be my rescuer. I truly disclaim your making me partner before." Surely the wrong-doers— for them is a painful chastisement. (14:22)

Shaitān tells us that we will become poor if we spend money in charity.[2:268] People who are in error think that this is a good advice. As a result many people do not like to give charity and do not pay their zakāt.

Shaitān threatens you with poverty, and bids you to indecency; while Allah promises you forgiveness from Himself and abundance. And Allah is ample-Giving, all-Knowing. (2:268)

Shaitān can control only those who listen to him.[15:42] If we do not respond, Shaitān cannot control us.

"Surely as to My servants you have no authority over them except him who, out of the misguided ones, follows you (i.e. Shaitān). (15:42)

Shaitān gives up his evil tricks with the people who are spiritually advanced.[15:40] This is similar to those people who have finished their university education, and no longer require tests.

False promise: The promise of Allāh (swt) is always true. Shaitān also makes promises, but these are never true.[4:120]

He promises them and raises vain desires in them. And Shaitān promises to them nothing but deception. (4:120)

His promises are traps. He is not scary but he shows scary situations[3:175] and promises to rescue people if they follow him. But he cannot be our rescuer.[14:22]

Shaitān is our enemy forever. While angels had submitted to Ādam, Iblīs the Shaitān refused to submit.[2:34] He was too arrogant. He claimed that he was superior because he was created out of Fire, while man was created out of Clay.[7:12]

Tribes of Shaitān: Shaitān is not a single entity, but they have their own tribes.[7:27] Human beings can also act as a Shaitān.[2:14] When people act as a hypocrite, they act like a Shaitān. Such people will tell you that they are Muslims, while they are not.[2:14]

And when they meet those who believe, they say: "We believe". But when they are alone with their Shaitān, they say: "We are really with you, we by ourselves were only mocking." (2:14)

Some people are ignorant about the majesty of Allāh (swt) but they argue about the existence of Allāh (swt).[22:3] These people act as Shaitān.

Protection from Shaitān: If Shaitān attacks us, we should seek refuge with Allāh (swt).[41:36]

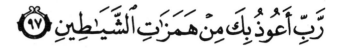

My Rabb! I take refuge with You— from the prompting of Shaitān (23:97)

It is advised that when we recite the Qur'ān, we should seek refuge from Shaitān. This is the way we can remain righteous.

So when you recite the Qur'ān, then you seek refuge with Allah from Shaitān, the driven away. (16:98).

Shaitān also tried misleading the nabis and the rasuls.[22:52] He engaged corrupt people against the nabis and the rasuls.[22:53] If we are on the right path, then the plot of the Shaitān remains weak.[4:76] Shaitān's reward will be in hellfire along with those who follow him.[7:18]

---

from hadith

It is reported that the Prophet (S) said: "Give charity without delay, for it stands in the way of calamity." (Al-Tirmidhī)

1. Read sūrah 38, verse 78. How long is the Shaitān condemned for his evil works?

    _____

2. Read sūrah An-Nahl (*The Bee*), verses 99 and 100, and then answer the following:

    a. Can Shaitān have control over those who believe in Allāh (swt)? _____

    b. Whom do Shaitān control? _____

    _____

    _____.

3. Read sūrah Sād, verses 82 and 83. Who cannot be misled by Shaitān?

    _____

4. What should we do before we read the Qur'ān? Find the answer in sūrah An-Nahl, verses 98.

    _____

5. Read sūrah Yā-Sīn, verse 60. Why did Allāh (swt) prohibit us from worshipping the Shaitān, the Evil-one?

    _____

6. Read sūrah Bani Isrā'īl, verse 63. What is the reward of the Shaitān and his followers?

    _____

Taqwā: *The Quality of True Believers*

Objective of the Lesson:

All Muslims are required to develop taqwā. If they do not exercise and develop taqwā his or her status as Muslim will be in jeopardy. This lesson describes what taqwā is and how we can develop taqwā in our mind and body.

When we declare Shahādah, we become Muslims. Once we are Muslim, we strive to be better at our spirituality. We can become better people by improving the level of our taqwā. A person who is practicing taqwā is trying to be a muttaqī.

Being a muttaqī is a step above being a Muslim. While all muttaqīs are Muslims, not all Muslims reach the level of a **muttaqī**. In this lesson we will analyze some of the important things that are we can do to become a muttaqī. With little practice and little initiative each one of us can start to become a muttaqī.

Taqwā: The word 'taqwā' comes from the root word of 'waqa', which means to save or to guard. Although there is no single English equivalent word, probably the closest meaning of taqwā is "to revere". Taqwā is also translated as "fearing Allāh", "keeping duty", "guarding against evil", etc. We have to fear Allāh, but this fear should be combined with a sense of sincere love. The closest example of taqwā could be the love of a child towards his or her parents. The children love their parents yet they are careful not to irritate or annoy them. They can approach their parents whenever they want to, but they know that they will be disciplined if they cross the boundary.

Importance of taqwā in Islam is so great that the Qur'ān and Sunnah of the Prophet (S) mentioned it numerous times. Everybody is required to practice taqwā. Everybody should become a muttaqī because the success in the Hereafter belongs to those who have taqwā. Therefore, remember it is not an item only for the Imam of the mosque or few good people.

Not a separate group: We should remember that muttaqī is not a separate group of people. They are not supposed to be different from the rest of the Muslims. In order to be a muttaqī you do not have to isolate yourself from all worldly things and become like a saint. You do not have to devote your life only in praying and only in fasting and do not have to become a person who abandons good things in life. In order to be a muttaqī you have to fear Allāh, look to what Allāh has ordered us to carry out and avoid doing anything that earns His displeasure and anger.

Command to have taqwā: In the Qur'ān several commands are given to all of us to have taqwā.

O you who believe! Have taqwā of Allah, and let a soul look to what it sends forward for the morrow. And revere Allah. Surely Allah is Aware of what you do. (59:18)

And compete with one another towards protection from your Rabb and a Garden whose breadth is as the heavens and the earth— prepared for the muttaqī. (3:133)

O you who believe! Sawm is prescribed for you, as it was prescribed to those who preceded you,— that you may practice reverence. (2:183)

In this verse fasting is prescribed for everyone. The purpose of fasting is to develop taqwā. Thus, everyone should work hard to develop taqwā. Fasting is one tool to develop taqwā, there are many other ways we can develop it.

Let us read three verses from Sūrah Al-Baqarah (2:3-5):

ٱلَّذِينَ يُؤْمِنُونَ بِٱلْغَيْبِ وَيُقِيمُونَ ٱلصَّلَوٰةَ وَمِمَّا رَزَقْنَٰهُمْ يُنفِقُونَ ۝ وَٱلَّذِينَ يُؤْمِنُونَ بِمَآ أُنزِلَ إِلَيْكَ وَمَآ أُنزِلَ مِن قَبْلِكَ وَبِٱلْءَاخِرَةِ هُمْ يُوقِنُونَ ۝ أُوْلَٰٓئِكَ عَلَىٰ هُدًى مِّن رَّبِّهِمْ وَأُوْلَٰٓئِكَ هُمُ ٱلْمُفْلِحُونَ ۝

who believe in the Unseen, and establish the salāt, and out of what We have provided them with, they do spend;

and who believe in what has been revealed to you, and in what was revealed before you, and regarding the Hereafter they firmly believe.

These are upon Guidance from their Rabb, and these are themselves the successful.

These three verses characterize a muttaqī:

• Who takes the Qur'ān as the Guide.

• Muttaqī believes in the *al-ghaib* or the Unseen. This belief is not based on blind faith, but after seeing the clear proof of the Unseen.

• Establishes the Salāt.

• Spends in good causes from what Allāh (swt) has provided.

• Believes in the revelation to Muhammad (S) and the earlier prophets, and

• Believes in the Hereafter.

While a person can become a Muslim within a minute by stating the Shahādah, becoming muttaqī is not a quick process. We have to persevere and practice taqwā.[3:125] We should develop and increase taqwā or awareness of Allāh (swt), since He created us,[4:1] and for the fact that He will cause us to die.[10:31] Even Rasulullah (S) was asked to practice taqwā.[33:1] His wives too were asked to practice taqwā.[33:32]

All prophets practiced taqwā: The concept of achieving taqwā is not limited to Muhammad (S) and his followers. All the previous prophets also asked their followers to practice taqwā. Ibrāhīm (A) told his people to revere Allāh (swt), because it was better.[29:16] So did 'Isā (A) tell his community.[5:112] Mūsā (A) reminded others that the finest ending of life is for those who are muttaqī.[7:128] Nūh[26:106], Ilyas[37:124], Sālih[26:142], Hūd[7:65], Lūt[26:161], Shu'aib[26:177] and other prophets, may peace be upon all of them, asked their people to revere Allāh (swt). As in the Qur'ān, the Injīl also contained guidance to

become muttaqī.[5:46]

How to achieve taqwā: There are many ways we can develop taqwā. If we follow the Qur'ān, then we can practice taqwā.[6:155] Staying on the right path brings us closer to taqwā.[5:2] Salāt[6:72] and fasting[2:183] are two great ways to practice taqwā. When we sacrifice an animal for the sake of Allāh (swt), the blood or meat do not reach Allāh (swt), but our piety reaches Him.[22:37] Eating permitted food and avoiding prohibited food are ways to develop taqwā.[5:88]

When we try to avoid sins, we are working towards taqwā.[5:2] Having a good relationship with other Muslims is a form of reverence.[49:10] Gift and charities for the sake of Islam is also a way to taqwā.[8:1] There are many good ways that we can practice to become a muttaqī. Our efforts to become honest is a good way to practice taqwā.[5:100]

Benefits of being a muttaqī: The benefits of being a muttaqī are many. Practicing taqwā and persevering bring us success. By following the Qur'ān and practicing reverence, we can expect mercy from Allāh (swt).[6:155] A person can avoid the hellfire by practicing taqwā.[39:16] Taqwā can take us to heaven,[6:32] since this is a promise of Allāh (swt) towards the Muttaqī.[13:35] Allāh (swt) helps the muttaqī against disbelievers.[9:123] On the Day of Judgment, the muttaqīs will be protected while the disbelievers will not.[9:72]

homework**weekend 23**

1. Write five different ways that you may practice taqwā:

    a. _____

    b. _____

    c. _____

    d. _____

    e. _____

2. In the space below, write the characteristics of a muttaqī:

    _____

    _____

    _____

    _____

3. Read Sūrah Yūnus, verse 63 and 64. What are the rewards of those who believe and practice reverence?

    a. _____

    b. _____

4. In the Hereafter, where will the muttaqīs be? Find the answer in Sūrah Al-Hijr (*The Rock*), verse 45.

    _____

5. In Sūrah Maryam, verse 13, a prophet is said to be a muttaqī. Find the name of the prophet from the previous verse.

    _____

My Friend is a Muslim Now

Objective of the Lesson:

In the West, many people are reverting and accepting Islam as their religion. This lesson, written from the viewpoints of two friends, describes the typical struggles and expectations of new Muslims.

Today I want to tell you about one of my friends, his name is Kevin. He is not my neighbor, but I know him very well. He goes to my school. We played soccer when we were in first grades. He was in my soccer team. Both he and I were two best players in the team.

Kevin's father is an engineer and his mother works at a medical office. About six months back Kevin's entire family accepted Islam. My friend Kevin is a Muslim now. Over the past six months my family has come to know Kevin and his family closely. Becoming Muslim was an easy choice, but the process that followed was sometimes difficult for them. It was a great sacrifice and a big commitment. I want to share with you something that I learned from my friend Kevin.

Appeal of the religion: These days, many people say bad things about Islam and Muslims. The media portrays the bad things that some Muslims do in the name of Islam. Kevin's father became curious about Islam in the past few years when Islam was a hot topic due to a national disaster. He began finding out about Islam and particularly about Muhammad (S) to understand the message of Islam. He realized that true Islam is much different and better than what he heard in the news and media.

Islam recognizes Jesus: Kevin's father was surprised to find that Jesus was a highly respected prophet in Islam. He was equally surprised that the Qur'ān mentioned about Jesus and Mary with dignity and honor. He read in the Qur'ān that Mary was respected as an honored woman in the world.[3:42] According to the Qur'ān, the birth, the death and the awakening of Jesus is a mark of honor for him.

Respect towards all religion: Kevin's father was surprised to find a few verses in the Qur'ān that say no matter what, if people believe in God and do good deeds they will be rewarded. He read in the verses 5:69 and 22:17 that those who follow religions like the Sabeans, Magian—the two past religions and those who are Jews and Christians— as long as they believe in God, do good deeds and believe in the Awakening, they have no fear. Kevin's father felt that Islam has to be truly a world religion since it is able to broaden its umbrella in this manner. Other religions say a person must believe in that faith and follow the messiah of the faith to get god's blessing. But Islam is not bound to such limited outlook.

Why new religion: Before accepting Islam, Kevin's father had difficulty in seeing Islam as a religion. To him, Christianity was the best religion for all the people. Then he realized that God had in the past

sent prophets like Abraham, Isaac, Jacob, Joseph, Moses, Jesus. God did not stop with Abraham or with Moses. He sent more prophets. Therefore, it was possible for God to send another prophet after

Jesus. In the Bible Jesus said unless he left, a new messenger would not come. Jesus said he could not say everything; the new messenger would clarify what he could not clarify. When Kevin's father related such messages from the Bible it made sense to him to believe that Muhammad (S) was the new messenger.

Conduct of Muhammad (S): Kevin's father was impressed when he read the biography of Muhammad (S). He was impressed by his sense of justice, equality, treatment of the poor, treatment of the women and treatment of fellow beings. Muhammad (S) was a virtual king of the Muslim empire, but he never acted as a king. He never exploited people to gain personal advantage. Kevin's father came to believe that truth about Muhammad (S) far above than what the western media tell about him.

Big sacrifice: People who give up their faith and accept Islam make many sacrifices. The biggest sacrifice is definitely giving up the values, teachings, principles with which they grew up. A person who associated deities with Allāh all his life and used to "seeing" his god in the form of figures, suddenly quits the concept of associating! It is a big jump for him. To believe God is unseen requires a lot of mental adjustment. Entire thinking of the person needs to be modified. He has to be careful not to associate anything or any concept with God. It is easy to say, but it is difficult for a person who just accepted Islam.

Then, there is adjustment at the social level. After accepting Islam, suddenly all the near and dear relatives treat him as an alien. They see the person as an "outcast." The person feels detached from social circles. He is viewed as a traitor. He is viewed as an evil and destined to the hell. To give up previous faith was a challenge, now to give up near and dear ones was traumatic. Kevin's father felt that many Muslims do not understand this aspect of sacrifice that a new Muslim goes through.

As a result there is a big disconnection between the new Muslims and born Muslims.

Sense of "not belonging": Kevin's family told us that after accepting Islam suddenly they felt they do not belong to any place. They wished born-Muslim people helped them feel more comfortable. They realized, suddenly many Muslims started giving

them too much advice, not realizing whether or not they can absorb everything so quickly. As if these Muslims wanted to make Kevin's family "perfect" Muslim in a single day. By doing this, they isolate the reverts, said Kevin's family.

Strong points of Islam: I asked Kevin and his family what they think were the strongest points about Islam. My idea was to know from him which point about Islam made them incline towards Islam. They told me the following:

- All men are equal in the sight of God.

- Men and women are equal in the sight of God.

- God is merciful, kind.

- You do not need any middle man to reach to God.

- Whoever does good and believes in One God can hope for God's mercy.

- God's mercy is not entirely for Muslims, everybody can hope for it.

- Everybody is responsible for his or her own action.

- God does not need any help or any family to manage His kingdom.

- Islam respects Jesus, Moses, Abraham and other biblical prophets.

- Islam recognizes the Bible and the Torah as books revealed by God.

- God of Islam is the same God Christians and Jews worship.

1. Read verse 5:82. Which group of people are said to be nearest in love with the believers?

_____

2. Kevin told his friend to read verse 22:78 from sūrah al-Hajj. Read the verse and answer the following:

    What has Allāh not imposed for us in the religion: _____

    The religion of Islam was preached by which '*father*'? _____

    Who has named all the people "Muslim"? _____

3. Who was sent as a mercy for the entire world? Find your answer by reading verse 21:107.

_____

4. In verse 3:85 Allāh says something will not be accepted from anybody. What will be accepted and what will not be accepted? Answer after reading the verse.

    Will be accepted: _____

    Will not be accepted: _____

5. When you meet a person who has accepted Islam recently, how would you welcome him in Islam. What would you tell him about being a Muslim?

_____

Friendship: *With Others and With People of Opposite Gender*

Objective of the Lesson:

As part of our daily life we build friendship with people of other faith. We need to exercise caution about who we befriend with. Good friends can make us good, and many so called "good" friends can destroy us. The students will learn what to look for when they make friends, and what type of friendship they should avoid.

All of us have friends. We have friends just like our parents have friends. We love to play with friends, talk to them, and invite them to our homes. Some of our friendships are short and others are long time friendship. When we leave school, we do not see most of our old friends anymore. In a new school we get new friends. Some of our friends are Muslims, some are Christian and some are from other faiths. We get along with friends but sometimes we have misunderstanding with friends. After a misunderstanding sometimes we become friends again. Sometimes we are not friends anymore. Sometimes we become friends with someone, but even without a misunderstanding we decide not to be friendly with that person anymore.

The reason we are studying friends and friendship in this lesson is because the Qur'ān and Sunnah of the Prophet (S) tells us what types of friends we should look for, who to have as friends and who to avoid.

Choose friends carefully: Not all friends are good friends. We have to be careful when we choose friends. Normally we think of good friends as those who have the following things in common with us:

- They share our happiness and sadness.
- They trust us and stay with us always.
- They stand by us.

Let us say James in your school is a bully. He is mean with everyone, he breaks things, damages school property and gets in trouble in the school. Let us say in the school there is another boy named Adam. He is also a bully - mean with others and gets in trouble in the school. But James and Adam are friends. Why not, they share happiness and sadness, they trust each other and stand by each other. Now look what happens to them—nobody likes them in school, they get in trouble in school and get bad grades in exams. In this example friends who stand by each other or share happiness and sadness are not the reason to befriend with. Not all friends who appear to be "good friends" are truly the friends you want in your life.

What to look for in friends: Islam says the only quality we should look for in a friend is if that friend is "righteous." This is the only criteria in a friend that is worthwhile in this life and in the Hereafter.

Friends who are not righteous need not become our enemy; we can still continue be good with them. We should be careful about what they do. They may give us advice that sounds good, but in reality it might be harmful for us. When it comes to taking advice from such friends, we should think twice. Some of their advice may be honest and good, but some may not be. We should discuss with our parents who can tell us if an advice of such a friend is truly good.

If your friend happens to be righteous, and if the same friend shares your happiness and sadness, remains loyal and trustful to you and stands by you, such friendship will be ideal.

Best friend is Allāh: We cannot see Allāh and we cannot play with Allāh. Yet, in the Qur'ān Allāh tells us that He is the best protecting friend of a true Muslim. The Arabic word indicating such

friendship is *walī*. He is the best protecting friend because He wants good for us. He protects us and guides us. He gives us rewards and He teaches us. His advice to us is the best advice. He never cheats us and He always keeps His promise. We can continue to have good friends, but at the same time we try to develop a friendship with Allāh. Such friendship with Allāh develops when we listen to Allāh and follow His command. Allāh said Ibrāhīm (A) was Allāh's friend because he listened to Allāh and followed His command. All prophets listened to Allāh and obeyed His command. Therefore Allāh protected all the prophets.

Friendship with Shaitān: Just as we do not see Allāh but can have friendship with Him, similarly we do not see Shaitān but sometimes he can pretend to be our friend. He whispers bad things in our hearts. He makes us believe that a bad thing is fun to do. He acts as if he is our good friend and acts as if he shares our thoughts and stands by us. But once he makes us do a bad thing and we begin to suffer, he walks away. He wants to destroy us by telling sweet things in our mind. In the Qur'ān, Allāh tells us that Shaitān is the enemy of the people. All bad people take Shaitān as their friend.

Friendship with Jews and Christians: The Qur'ān has not prohibited us from making friendship with the Jews or the Christians. There are many good people among them. Sometimes they are our good neighbors.

The Qur'ān tells us if anybody wants to harm us, or drive us out of our homes, or our country, or fights with us, we should not take such people as our friends. During the time of the Prophet (S) some Jews and Christians were fighting against the Muslims and wanted to kill them. They wanted to kill our Prophet (S). At that time Allāh told Muslims should not make friendship with the Jews and the Christians, who fight against the Muslims.

Friendship between boys and girls: Most of us go to schools where boys and girls are in the same class. Many of the boys have girls in the neighborhood as their friends, and many girls have boys in the neighborhood who are their friends. Islam requires us to be very careful about friendship between boys and girls, especially when they are growing up. You can talk to boys or girls without touching each other. You should not play games where you have to touch each other. Any activity between boys and girls should be in the presence of their parents or an elderly person. A boy and a girl should not be alone in a room. If you have to sit down and talk to each other, make sure you sit separate from each other. This is an Islamic manner. Islam does not say boys and girls should hate each other, but it wants them to maintain decency and modesty.

from**hadith**

It is narrated that Prophet Muhammad (S) once said: "A person is likely to follow the faith of his friend, so look whom you befriend."

1. According to the lesson, when we make friendship what three things become common among friends?

    (a) _____

    (b) _____

    (c) _____

2. Explain why the three things you mentioned in question 1 above can be misleading when we try to make friends.

_____

_____

3. The Qur'ān does not prohibit us from making friends with people of other faiths. But under three circumstances we should not make friendship with them. What are the three circumstances?

    (a) _____

    (b) _____

    (c) _____

4. Allāh says He is the *walī* of the Muslims. What is meant by the term *walī*?

_____

5. In verse 24:30 Allāh said the believing men should do two things. What are the two things?

    (a) _____

    (b) _____

6. How does the instruction in 24:30 be applied when boys and girls make friendship with each other? Explain your answer.

_____

_____

'Reading' Salāt or Performing Salāt

Objective of the Lesson:

This lesson continues to encourage students to perform salāt on regular basis. Often salāt is "read" or "observed" for the sake of it. Students will learn why they need to perform salāt. True performance of salāt has many benefits in the physical and spiritual wellbeing of the Muslim.

Throughout the Qur'ān Allāh has repeatedly told us to perform salāt. Islam has five pillars, of which salāt is the second pillar. Salāt is the cornerstone of being a righteous person. If a person does not embrace salāt in his or her daily life it will seriously damage his or her chances of getting reward in the Hereafter. Importance of salāt was discussed in detail in a lesson in 5th grade.

In this lesson we are going to cover how to perform salāt. We are not going to cover the steps of salāt as all of you should know the steps. If you need to review the steps of salāt, you may check the Appendix in the book. In this lesson we will discuss how you should devote and dedicate your salāt.

Reading salāt: To many of us salāt is just a ritual. A ritual is a religious duty we do by following some laws. Sometimes a ritual becomes a mechanical process or a robotic action. We do a ritual because we have to do it, but we do not understand the value of the ritual. We often "do" salāt but do not perform it. We look around, our minds roam about, we move in salāt, we push someone standing by our side. Sometimes you will hear some children giggle during salāt. We read a few sūrah very hurriedly. We go through the steps of salāt as if we are in a competition as to who can finish it first. Sometimes we do it just to make our parents happy. We spend hours watching TV or playing a game or browsing the Internet. But when it comes to "performing" salāt, we end up "reading" salāt without paying any attention.

Salāt is a worship of our Creator: We often forget that salāt is a form of worshipping our Creator. Worshipping our Creator does not require a lot of time. Most of the fard or compulsory part of the salāt can be performed in four to five minutes without rushing through it. We worship our Creator as a mark of our submission to Him. We worship Him five times a day to make frequent connection and a sense of submission to him. In return for showing our submission to our Creator, we earn reward. Such rewards will count in our favor in the Hereafter.[2:277]

Meeting an important person: If one day the governor of our state comes to our school, imagine how excited we will be. All of us will be quiet and extra careful to show respect to the governor. We will be well behaved so that the governor gets a good opinion about our school. If we stand in front

of him, we will show him respect and talk to him in a nice manner. We will be attentive to him. If we have to say something to him, we will speak carefully. Now in place of the governor, if the president of the country comes to our school, we will show even more respect and honor.

Allāh is the President of all the presidents. He is the Governor of all the governors. In salāt we stand before Allāh. We should show much more respect, dedication, attention during salāt. Allāh told us salāt restrains us from shameful conduct and unjust deeds.[29:45]

Humility to be shown in salāt: Humility means modesty and humbleness. When we perform salāt we should try to be humble because we are worshipping our Creator. If we stand in a careless and unmindful way we are not humble. True believers show humbleness during salāt.[23:2] Allāh told us to stand in salāt with devotion.[2:238] How can we show devotion if we are not attentive and humble?

Aqimus Salāh: In many verses Allāh told us to aqimus salāh or to establish salāh. Allāh did not use the word "read" or "do" the salāh. To establish salāt requires our commitment, time and sincerity. We can only establish something if we are careful about it. We cannot establish anything if we are unmindful.

Performance of salāt increases piety: The word piety means goodness or piousness of our mind. If we are simply reading salāt like a robot, we cannot expect to increase our piety.

Practice to become humble: Before starting a salāt if we remind ourselves that we are going to stand before our Lord, we can be much more humble. We can try to remind ourselves that we will not be unmindful. We should try to give utmost attention to salāt. Modesty and humbleness in prayer will not come in one day. We have to keep trying. If we try, Allāh will help us.

homework**weekend 26**

1. Read verse 2:238. In this verse Allāh tells us to be obedient during salāt. But He also tells to do something about salāt. What is that?

_____

2. Past prophets also performed salāt. Read 10:87; 14:40 and 19:31 and write the names of the prophets who performed salāt.

   10:87—Salāt performed by: _____

   14:40—Salāt performed by: _____

   19:31—Salāt performed by: _____

3. In verse 23:1 Allāh says success belongs to the Mu'minūn or the believers. Then in the next verse Allāh mentions about one of the qualities of the believers. What does the 2nd verse say about the quality of the believers and what should they do?

_____

4. Read Sūrah Al-'Ankabut (*the Spider*), verse 45. Then answer the following:

   a. Salāt restrains us from _____ and _____

5. What should the state of our mind be when we are praying salāt? Find the answer in 2:238.

_____

6. If we are in danger, we may pray salāt in two ways. Read verse 2:239 to answer the two ways:

   (a) _____ (b) _____.

Muslims Around the World

Objective of the Lesson:

Muslims are spread all over the world. They have different culture, ethnicity, language, nationality—but they are all tied together through the bond of Islam. In the world about 80% Muslims are non-Arab. The largest Muslim country by population is Indonesia. All these facts give interesting perspective about Muslims. This lesson shows there is unity in diversity among Muslims.

In the world there are about 6.6 billion people. Of these 6.6 billion people, about 1.4 billion people are Muslims. This means every sixth person in the world is a Muslim. All these Muslims are scattered all over the word. This number is rapidly increasing. More and more people are accepting Islam. Their spread all over the world makes Islam truly a world religion.

Early Muslims in Arabia: Islam first came in Arabia. During the first thirteen years of the Prophet's life in Makkah, there were about 70 Muslims. After the Prophet (S) migrated to Madīnah, the number of Muslims continued to increase. By the time the Prophet (S) conquered Makkah in 628 C.E., the number of Muslims increased to well over 10,000 people. After the Prophet (S) conquered Makkah, very soon the number of Muslims increased to over 100,000. Within one hundred years of Islam, entire Arabia, Persia and a large part of North Africa came under Islamic rule and hundreds of thousands of people became Muslim. Largest number of people who became Muslim in the early years were not born Muslims, but people who accepted Islam as their way of life.

Number of Muslims in Saudi Arabia: Present day Saudi Arabia is the land where the Prophet (S) was born and preached Islam. Today Saudi Arabia has total population of about

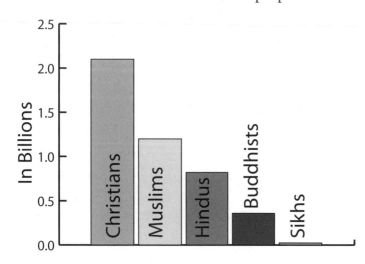

27.6 million. Almost all of them are Muslims. This means Muslims in Saudi Arabia represent 2% of total Muslims in the whole world. If all the Muslims in Saudi Arabia, Syria, Jordan, Palestine are combined, they represent about 5% of all Muslims in the world.

Largest Muslim country: Indonesia has the largest number of Muslims. It has total 231 million people of Muslims. It has about 8.5 times more Muslims than Muslims in Saudi Arabia. The second largest Muslim population is in Pakistan.

Majority of the Muslims are minority: Ironically, majority of the Muslims are minority in some country. In India, there are 120 million Muslims, larger than the Muslim population in Saudi Arabia, yet Muslims in India are a minority. They represent about 11% of the total population. In China there are about 26 million Muslims. They are all minority in that country. In the US, the Muslims are clearly a minority. In entire Europe, we can find Muslims in every country, but everywhere they are minority. In some European countries there are a sizeable Muslim population, e.g. Great Britain, France, Germany, Italy, Finland, yet they are minority in each country. In Australia Muslims are minority.

15 MUSLIM COUNTRIES		
1 Indonesia	231.6	million
2 Pakistan	163.6	million
3 Bangladesh	158.6	million
4 Nigeria	148.0	million
5 Egypt	75.0	million
6 Turkey	74.8	million
7 Iran	71.2	million
8 Sudan	38.5	million
9 Algeria	33.8	million
10 Morocco	31.2	million
11 Iraq	28.9	million
12 Uzbekistan	27.3	million
13 Saudi Arabia	27.6	million
14 Afghanistan	27.1	million
15 Malaysia	27.1	million

Language of the Muslims: The language of the Qur'ān is Arabic. The language of the majority of the Muslims in the world is not Arabic. Muslims in different parts of the world speak different languages. A Chinese Muslim speaks in Mandarin or other languages of China. A Bangladeshi Muslim speaks Bangla. A Somalian Muslim speaks in Somali. Many of them do not speak, write or understand Arabic. Yet all of them are guided by the Qur'ān and the sunnah of the Prophet (S).

Cultural diversity: The Muslims living in different countries are ethnic groups of that country or region. Each ethnic group has its own culture, tradition and food habit. They adopt or maintain the local culture or tradition as long as these do not conflict with the true teachings of Islam. Sometimes their culture and tradition is determined by the teachings of Islam. A Muslim will never adopt a culture that is against the teachings of Islam. But they have no hesitation in maintaining local tradition. For this reason, Muslims in many countries like India, Sri Lanka, Malaysia, Korea etc. are truly native people of the respective countries and they are never viewed as "outsiders." During early years of Islam when the Muslims migrated to different countries, they settled in those countries and adopted the respective countries as their own. They married local people and adopted local language. Eventually after a few generations the immigrant Muslims became fully blended with the local people.

Unity in diversity: Although the Muslims in the world speak different languages and have different ethnicity and culture, they are tied together by the bond of Islam. They follow the same Qur'ān and follow the guidance of the Prophet (S). Although they read translations of the Qur'ān in their languages, nobody wants to replace the Arabic Qur'ān. They never fail to recite the Arabic Qur'ān. Thousands of non-Arabic speaking people have memorized the Qur'ān. As a sign of unity, all the Muslims go to Makkah for Hajj.

1. Which country has the largest number of Muslim population?

_____

2. What is true about majority of the Muslims in the world?

    (a)   The majority of the Muslims are African American
    (b)   The majority of the Muslims are Chinese.
    (c)   The majority of the Muslims are minority in some country.
    (d)   The majority of the Muslims do not pray.

3. The Muslims in the world have different language, culture and tradition. What two things shows unity in their diversity?

    (a) _____

    (b) _____

4. Wherever the Muslims migrated, they did something in the new land. Which of the following choice is correct about them?

    (a)   They killed the local people and occupied their land.
    (b)   They adopted the land as their own.
    (c)   They forced the local people to speak in Arabic.
    (d)   They oppressed the local people.

5. Survey your class about the languages some of the students speak at home. Mention how many different languages your class friends can speak.

_____

6. **Project assignment:** Students will prepare a world map showing Muslim population in some of the major countries in the world in all continents. Color the map as far as possible. Submit the map for grading and displaying in the hallway of the school.

People of Other Faiths

Objective of the Lesson:

We live with people of other faiths. This lesson discusses what the other faiths are, how the people from other faith worship and how they are identical or different from the Muslims. The students will learn about the faiths in order to get a fair idea about them. This knowledge will help them appreciate their own religion and respect the religion of other people.

We live in a country where there are many different types of people. In the USA the exact number of Muslim population was not determined. It is estimated that about 2% of the people or approximately 6 million people are Muslims. Clearly the majority of the people in the USA are not Muslim.

At your regular school in the USA you may be the only Muslim student in your class. But in some schools there could be many Muslim students in one class. The same thing is true about the neighborhood you live in. Your family may be the only Muslim family in the neighborhood, but there may be other Muslim families round the block. In Europe and Australia, the scenario is quite different as many cities have much larger Muslim population.

Since we live in such a diverse society, it is a good idea to know about the people who live in the society. One way to know about them is to talk with them and be friendly with them. By becoming friendly with them you can learn about their values, culture, language, religion and many other things.

Today in this lesson we will study about the faith of other people who live in our neighborhood or who are in school or at work with us. Most of the people in our society are Christians. There are quite a few Jewish and Hindu people. Also you will find Buddhist people in

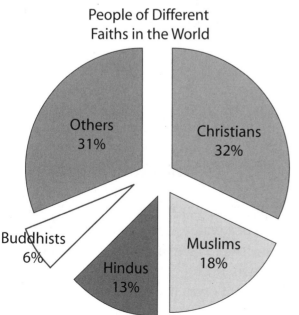

People of Different Faiths in the World

some neighborhoods as well as people who follow other smaller religions.

Common thing about all religions: The most common thing about all religion is their "faith." Faith is a unique system of belief. All religions have a unique system of belief. For example, we Muslims believe in a system that tells us Allāh is one, Muhammad (S) is our messenger, the Qur'ān is our holy book and so on. This system is our faith. We have not seen Allāh or Muhammad (S), but we trust them and believe in them. We do this because this is our faith.

Similarly other people from other religions have their own faith. They cannot prove many things just like we cannot prove many things about our religion, but they have faith just as we have faith. Because we have faith in Islam, therefore we are Muslim. Similarly because others have faith in Jesus Christ and the Bible, therefore they are Christian. Yet others have faith in the Torah and God Yahweh, therefore they are Jews.

Another most common thing about all religion is their faith in "god." Each religion has their god. They love their god and worship their god. However, the name, title, duty and gender of god in different religions is different. Also, the number of god in different religions is different. Only the Muslims and Jews believe there is One God. We

The Christians believe in One God but also believe in Jesus as Son of God. They often mention Jesus as Lord. They believe Jesus has divine power and they worship him. They also believe in Spirit or Angel Gabriel has some godly nature in him. Since they believe in more than one god, they are not monotheistic, but they are **polytheistic religion.** The word poly means more than one or many. Since they believe in threefold representation of god, they believe in the **Trinity**.

The Hindus believe in One God but they also believe in thousands of other gods. Therefore, they are also polytheistic people. All other major religions in the world practice polytheism or belief in multiple gods.

Difference between Islam and other religion: All major religions except Islam and Judaism believe in idols. These religions see their gods in the form of idols. Some of the idols have human form, some have strange human look-alike form and some have animal form. Many other idols have shapes of different objects. Some of the idols are human being e.g. Jesus, Zeus, Buddha, Rama, Aphrodite, Zarathustra etc. Other are objects created by Allāh but people mistakenly, consider them to be gods, e.g, the sun, the moon, wind, rain etc.

How do they worship: Every religion has their unique way of worship. In Islam we have formal

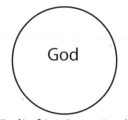

Belief in One God

Belief in three gods

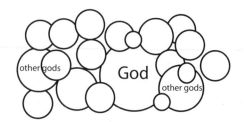

Belief in many gods

Muslims call our God Allāh. The Jews call their God Yahweh. Because we believe in one God, we believe in **monotheism** and our faith is called **monotheistic faith**. The word mono means one and theism means belief in god.

worship like salāt, sawm, etc. but we also have a broad view of worship. Every good work we do is a form of worship. For example, charity is worship, helping others is also worship. But none of these broad views of worship can substitute for the formal worship.

People from other faith worship in many different ways. Most of these ways are fixed, but sometimes different forms of worship are acceptable. For example the Christians go to the church on Sundays to worship. They do not have a daily prayer system like the Muslims. The nature and style of worship is different. It mostly includes reading passages from the Bible, singing songs of praise for Jesus and god, listening to the speech of the pastor and praying to god.

The Jews go to synagogue on Saturdays to pray. They too do not have any daily prayer system.

Hindus have many different forms of worship. They may pray to their idol at home or go to their temple and pray. The prayer time is not fixed. Anybody can go to the temple anytime and pray. Sometimes community prayer is arranged—but it is usually about listening to the talks of a priest. Among Hindus there are many different methods of prayer. Some are only for men, some are only for women and some are for everybody.

Basic belief: The Christians believe that for someone to go to Heaven, they must believe in Jesus as Son of God. They think only Christians will go to Heaven. The Jews believe only Jewish people will go to Heaven. For the Jews the present life is most important, the afterlife is not very important. The Hindus believe in many different things. They believe in rebirth for seven times. If one continues to do good work in each of the seven rebirths, ultimately they can go to Heaven. The Buddhists believe the soul of human being should achieve salvation or relief from the body. They do not have a clear idea about Heaven. For them the freedom of soul is most important.

Religious books: The religious book of the Christians is the Bible. It has two parts in it—the **Old Testament** and the **New Testament**. The religious books of the Jews are the **Torah** and the **Talmud**. Torah was revealed by Allāh. Talmud is their law book, written by Rabbis. The main religious book of the Hindus is **Gita**, but they also have many other books and each of them have several volumes. Most Hindus never read the religious books. Women are not allowed to touch Gita. The main religious book of the Buddhist is **Tripitak.** They too have many different books.

Common values: All religions have several common values in them. All religions prohibit lying, stealing, murder and many other types of social or criminal crime. All religions have many good values. You know why? All religions that came before Prophet Muhammad (S) were sent by Allāh. People followed the religion and later changed the religion to suit their needs. When they changed the religion, Allāh sent a new prophet to guide them to the right path or to bring them back to the original religion. For example, all religions have fasting as a required form of worship. The way the people fast in other religions are very different from our fasting because they changed their rules.

We should remember we live in a society that has people from other faith. Allāh says the only religion acceptable to Allāh is Islam, but we should not look down upon the people of other faiths. We believe ultimately each person is responsible for his or her own action. Allāh will judge each person based on the amount of good work and level of faith.

homework**weekend 28**

1. Define the term monotheism in a short sentence.

_____

2. Name two faiths that worship one God.

_____

3. What is polytheism?

_____

4. What is the main difference between Islam and polytheistic religions?

_____

5. Connect the words in two columns by drawing a line.

Gita	Buddhism
Old Testament	Hindu
Tawrat	Bible
Tripitak	Jews

6. Which of the following choices is correct about all religions?

    (a)   All religions worship only one God.
    (b)   All religions have some common values.
    (c)   All religions worship multiple gods.
    (d)   All religions were changed by people to suit their needs.

7. Read verse 3:85. Which religion is mentioned as acceptable to God?

_____

8. Read verse 3:19. Who do you think changed the Books due to mutual jealousy?

_____

Appendix

Steps of Salāt

The description provided in these pages is the commonly accepted way of performing salāt in Hanafi madhhab. There may be minor variations, which are allowed. All the variations should have supporting proof that Rasulullah (S) had occasionally practiced that variation. The teacher/parents are requested to show the ideal practice according to their madhab. The salāh has to be made in Arabic language only.

Physical preparation for salāt:

Physical cleanliness: Before performing salāt, make sure you have a clean body. You must do Wūdū, and be in the state of wūdū. At any time during the salāt, do not look sideways, do not look at others, do not talk to others in the middle of the salāt. Do not make unnecessary movements. Do not scratch, yawn, laugh or smile. If you must sneeze or cough, that is Okay, but try to minimize it.

Clean clothes: Your clothes should be clean and should cover the body. For boys, the clothes should cover at least from the naval to the knees. For girls, the clothes should cover from the neck to the ankle, and to the wrist. The head is covered, while face can remain uncovered. Clothes should not be see-through or transparent. Avoid any clothing that has picture of people, animals or bad writings.

Clean place: You should find a clean place to make your salāt. A prayer rug is not necessary. A prayer rug should be kept clean to make sure you are praying on a clean place.

Direction: During salāt you have to face the *Qiblah*, which is the direction of Ka'bah in Makkah.

Time: Fard (compulsory) prayers are performed at the proper and appointed time. It is preferable to perform the prayer as soon as the Adhan (call to prayer) is announced.

Mental preparation: We should begin the prayer with full mental and physical attention. During salāt, we are directly talking to Allah, therefore we must be attentive. Avoid any place or object that can divert your attention.

What is a raka'ah?

Each salāt can be divided into cycles of physical postures or raka'at. Each raka'ah involves position of qiyam (standing), ruku, (bowing), sujud (prostration), jalsa (seated), and again a sujud (prostration), and associated recitations. Following are the specified raka'at in the five daily salāt. Some variation on the number of Sunnah prayer exists among the madhhab.

	Sunnah raka'at before Fard raka'at	Fard raka'at	Sunnah raka'at after Fard raka'at
Fajr	2	2	
Dhuhr	4	4	2
'Asr	4	4	
Maghrib		3	2
'Isha	4	4	2, then 3 (wajib)

Description of a 2 raka'at salāt:

The following description is for a salāt of two raka'at (e.g. Fard prayer of Fajr). At the end the description, there is a brief note on how to perform 3 or 4 raka'at of salāt.

Step 1

Make an intention to perform the salāt for the sake of Allāh. Say to yourself (in any language) that you intend to offer this salāt (Fajr, Dhuhr, Asr, Maghrib or Isha), Fard, Sunnat or Witr, and the number of rakahs (example—"I intend to offer two Rakah of Fard, Fajr prayer for Allāh").

Position: *qiyam.* Stand upright. Raise both hands up to the ears (palms facing the *Qiblah, —the direction to Ka'bah*)

What to say: *"Allāhu Akbar"* (Allāh is the Greatest).

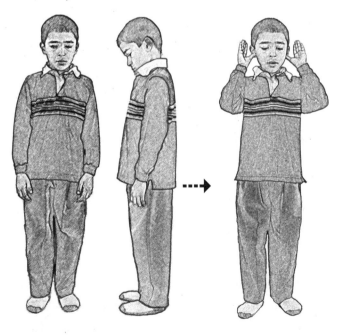

Step 2

Position: Place your left hand over your stomach, and then place your right hand on top of the left hand, and grip around the wrist of the left hand.

What to say:

1. *"Subhanaka Allāhumma wa bihamdika, wa tabārakasmuka, wa ta'āla jadduka, wa lā ilāha ghairuka".* (This part is known as Thana (or Sana). It means "Glory be to you O Allāh, and praise to You. Blessed be Your Name, exalted be Your Majesty and Glory. There is no god but You")

2. *"A'ūdu billāhi mina ash-Shaytānir rajim"* (I seek protection of Allāh against Shaitan, the condemned)

3. *"Bismillāhir rahmānir rahīm"* (In the Name of Allāh, Most Gracious, Most Merciful.)

4. Then recite Sūrah Al-Fātihah. It is a must to recite Sūrah Al-Fātihah in each raka'ah. A salāt is not valid if Sūrah Al-Fātihah is not recited while praying alone.

"Al humdu li-llahi rabbi-l 'alamīn. Ar-rahmāni-r rahīm. Māliki yawmi-d dīn. Iyyāka na'budu wa iyyāka nasta'īn. Ihdina-s sirāta-l mustaqīm. Sirātal ladhīna an'amta 'alaihim, ghairil maghdūbi 'alaihim, wa la-d dāllīn. (Āmīn)"

(The Praise belong to Allāh, The Rabb of all

the worlds; the Rahman; the Rahim. Malik of the Day of Judgment. You alone do we serve, and to You alone we seek for help. Guide us on the Right Path, —the path of those upon whom You have bestowed favors; not of those upon whom wrath is brought down, nor those gone-astray.)

5. After reciting surah Fātihah, we will now recite any short sūrah or a few verses from the Holy Qur'ān. This additional recitation of a part of the Qur'ān is done in the first two rakah only. We should recite the sections in the order that they appear in the Qur'an, e.g. if you are going to recite sūrah Falaq and sūrah Nās in your prayer, you recite sūrah Falaq in the first rakah, and sūrah Nās in the second rakah. It is good to memorize as many sūrah as you can, as you can recite them in your salāt.

Step 3

What to say: *"Allāhu Akbar"*

Position: This position is called *Ruku.* First raise your hands up to your ears, then bow with your back perpendicular to your legs. In some variations, you are not required to raise

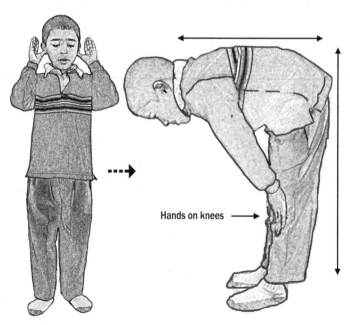

Hands on knees →

your hands up to you ears. Put your hands on your knees. Do not bend the knees.

What to say: *"Subhana rabbiyal 'Azīm"* (say it 3 times) (Glorified is my Rabb, the Great).

Step 4

While going back to *qiyam* (upright) position,

What to say: *"Samia Allahu liman hamidah"* (Allāh listens to him who praises Him)
Position: In *qiyam* position.

What to say: *"Rabbanā wa laka al hamd"* ("Our Rabb, praise be for You only")

Step 5

What to say: While going to the next position of sujud, say *"Allāhu Akbar"*

Position: This position is *sujud.* Place both your knees on the floor. Try not to move the position of your feet., i.e. do not step your feet away from the position of qiyam. After placing your knees down, then place your two hands on the ground, with your palms touching the ground. Do not glide your hands on the ground. Your elbow is away from the floor. The hands will be sufficiently apart to give space for your head. Now you will place your forehead on the floor. Both your nose and forehead should touch the ground. Your hands should be on the side of your head. Your stomach should not touch the floor. You should be most humble in this position.

The most powerful part of our body is our brain, the site of our intelligence. We submit our full selves, with full understanding, to Almighty Allāh. We should realize that our strength, power, wealth, everything that we have is from Allāh only. To confirm this physical and spiritual humbleness, we should repeat the sujud again in Step 7.

What to say: *"Subhana rabbiyal A'ala"* (say it 3 times) (Glory be to Allāh, the Exalted).

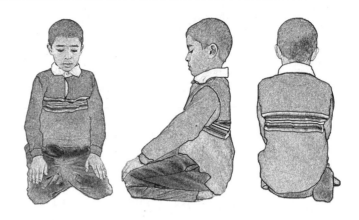

Rabb, forgive me and have Mercy on me).

Step 7

We will repeat the *sujud* again. Every rakah has two *sujud*.

What to say: While going to the position of sujud, say *"Allāhu Akbar"*

Position: *Sujud.* Place your palms on the floor, then place your forehead. Both the nose and forehead should touch the floor.

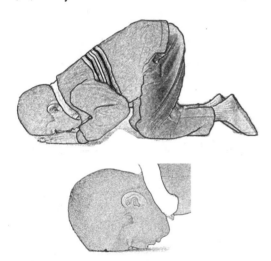

What to say: *"Subhāna rabbiyal A'ala"* (say it 3 times) (Glory be to Allāh, the Exalted".)

This completes one raka'ah

Step 6

The next position is *jalsa*.

What to say: While going to the *Jalsa* position, say *"Allāhu Akbar"*

Position: To go to jalsa position, rise from *sujud*. First raise your head off the floor, then raise your hands. Now you are sitting on the floor, this posture is called *Jalsa*.

What to say: *"Rabbi-ghfir li wa rhamni"* (O my

Beginning of second raka'ah

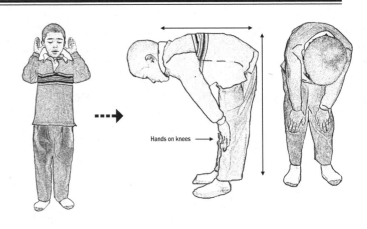

Hands on knees →

Step 8

You will rise to *qiyam* (upright) position. The movement should be in a systematic, graceful manner. First raise your forehead from the floor, then raise your hands off the ground, then you will raise your knees. Try not to move your feet, i.e., the position of your feet should be in the same place as it was in the first raka'ah.

What to say: While going up to the position of qiyam, say *"Allāhu Akbar"*

Position: You are standing upright. Hold the left hand with the right hand on top.

What to say:
1. *Surah Al-Fātihah*, and
2. Any short sūrah or some verses of the Holy Qur'ān.

Step 9

What to say: *"Allāhu Akbar"*

Position: *ruku*. Raise both hands up to the ear, palm facing the Qiblah. Bow with your back perpendicular to your legs. Put your hands on knee.

What to say: *"Subhāna rabbiyal 'Azīm"* (say it 3 times)

Step 10

Position: While going back to *qiyam* (upright) position,

What to say: *"Sami'a Allāhu liman hamidah"*

Position: In qiyam position. You are upright.

What to say: *"Rabbanā wa lakal hamd"*

Step 11

What to say: While going to the next position of sujud, say *"Allāhu Akbar"*

Position: *sujud*. Follow the sequence as in Step 5.

What to say: *"Subhāna Rabbiyal A'ala"* (say it 3 times)

Step 12

What to say: While going to the next position of *Jalsa*, say *"Allāhu Akbar"*

Position: Rise from the *Sujud* position. Now you are sitting in *Jalsa* position.

What to say: *"Rabbi-ghfir lī wa rhamnī"* (O my Rabb, forgive me and have Mercy on me).

Step 13

What to say: While going to the next position of sujud, say *"Allāhu Akbar"*

Position: *sujud.* Place your hands, and then place your forehead on the floor.

What to say: *"Subhāna Rabbiyal A'ala"* (say it 3 times).

Step 14

What to say: While going to the next position of *Jalsa*, say *"Allāhu Akbar"*

Position: Rise from the *Sujud* position. Now you are sitting on *Jalsa* position.

What to say:

"At-tahiyātu lillahi was-salawātu wattaiyibātu. Assalāmu 'alayka ayyuhan-

nabiyu wa rahmatullāhi wa barakātuhu. Assalāmu 'alainā wa 'ala 'ibadi-llāhis-sālihīn. Ashhadu an lā ilāha illallāhu wa ashhadu anna Muhammadan 'abduhu wa rasūluhu."

(All the salutations, prayers and nice things are for Allāh. Peace be on you O Prophet, and the blessings of Allāh, and His grace. Peace on us and on all the righteous servants of Allāh. I bear witness that none but Allāh is worthy of worship and bear witness that Muhammad is the servant and messenger of Allāh.) This is known as *Tashahud.*

(**Position:** raise your right index finger up while reciting the last part of this prayer)

Then recite the *Durūd.*

"Allāhumma salli 'ala Muhammadin wa 'ala āli Muhummadin, kamā sallayta 'ala Ibrāhima, wa ala āli Ibrāhima, innaka hamidun majid. Allāhumma barik 'ala Muhammadin wa 'ala āli Muhummadin, kama barakta ala Ibrāhima, wa 'ala āli Ibrahīm, innaka hamīdun majīd".

(O Allāh, send your Mercy on Muhammad and his followers as you sent Your mercy on Ibrahim and his followers. You are the Most Praised, The Most Glorious. O Allāh, send your Blessings on Muhammad and his followers as you have blessed Ibrahim and his followers. You are the Most praised, The Most Glorious.)

You may add a short prayer, such as:

"Rabbanā ātinā fi-d dunyā hasanatan wa fi-l ākhirati hasanatan, wa qinā ʿadhāban nār"

(Our Rabb, give us the good of this world, and good in the Hereafter and save us from the chastisement of Fire.)

There are other duʿā that you may learn and recite.

Step 15

Position: Slowly turn the face to the right. This is called salam

What to say: *"As-salāmu ʿalaikum wa rahmatullāh"* (Peace and mercy of Allāh be on you).

Step 16

Position: Slowly turn the face to the left. This is called salam

What to say: *"As-salāmu ʿalaikum wa rahmatullāh."*

This completes two raka'at of Salāh.

How to pray three raka'ats (Maghrib)

In order to perform a three raka'at salāh, all the postures and the prayers are the same up to step 13. But this time in step 14, recite up to *"At-tahiyātu lillahi was-salawātu wattaiyibātu. Assalāmu ʿalayka ayyuhan-nabiyu wa rahmatullāhi wa barakātuhu. Assalāmu ʿalainā wa ʿala ʿibadi-llāhis-sālihīn. Ashhadu an lā ilāha illallāhu wa ashhadu anna Muhammadan ʿabduhu wa rasūluhu."*

This is known as *Tashahud*. Saying *Allāhu akbar*, return back to the *qiyam* position, step 8. This time recite only *Al-Fātihah*, (in step 8) alone without adding any sūrah of the Qur'ān. Then all prayers and postures are the same as shown from step 9 - 16.

How to pray four raka'ats (Dhuhr, 'Asr and 'Isha)

In order to perform four raka'at prayer, all the postures and the prayers are the same up to step 13. In Step 14 only the prayer of *"Tashahud* will be recited, and the *qiyam* position, step 8, will be resumed. In position 8 recite only *Al-Fātihah* alone without adding any sūrah. Step 8 - 13, completes the third raka'ah. The *qiyam* position, step 8, will be re-assumed. In position 8 recite only *Al-Fātihah* without adding any sūrah. Step 8 - 16, completes the fourth raka'ah.

Prayer Postures

  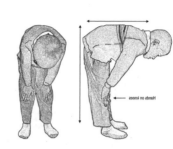 

Standing for salāt facing the direction of Ka'bah.

Front and lateral view

Rasing hands for takbir. Folding them back to recite sūrah.

Bending position for ruku.

Front and lateral view

Raising from ruku.

Performing sujud.

Sitting down from sujud, jalsa position.

Front, lateral and back view

Second sujud from jalsa position.

At the end of 2nd raka'at, sitting down after 2nd sujud to recite tashahud.

Completing salāt - turning face first to the right and then to the left.

Test Your Knowledge - 1
(All questions are based on the lessons taught in the book)

1. What is the general Arabic term for the most beautiful names of Allāh?

2. Who was one of the most renowned sahābah who wrote down the Qur'ān after it was revealed to the Prophet Muhammad (S)?

3. Which khalifa circulated the official copies of the Qur'ān and burned all private copies?

4. What is the meaning of the term Sahih Sittah?

5. Who was the most famous complier of Hadīth?

6. Name the six famous collectors of Hadīth.

7. Who was the king of the Israelites immediately before Dāwūd became their king?

8. Which prophet killed Jālūt or Goliath?

9. Which prophet sent a letter to the queen of Sheba?

10. After Mūsā ran away from Egypt, where did he settled down and married?

11. What is the meaning of Allāh's qualitative name al-Fattāh?

12. When infant Mūsā was rescued from the river, who found a nursing woman for him?

13. What is the name of the sūrah where first 5 revealed verses were compiled?

14. What is the plural form of the word Hadīth?

15. Which two persons in Nūh's family did not believe in Allāh?

Answer:

1. Asma al Husna
2. Zaid Ibn Thabit
3. Khalīfa 'Uthman ibn 'Affān
4. Six correct books of Hadīth
5. Imam Bukhārī
6. Imam Bukhārī, Imam Muslim, Ibn Mājāh, Abu
Dawūd, Tirmidhī and Nasā'ī
7. Tālūt
8. Dāwūd
9. Sulaimān
10. Madyan
11. The Opener
12. His sister
13. Al-'Alaq
14. Ahādīth
15. His wife and his son

Test Your Knowledge - 2

(All questions are based on the lessons taught in the book)

1. Which prophet appointed Tālūt as the king of Israelites?

2. What was the name of the queen who ruled over Sheba?

3. How old was Khadījah when she married Muhammad (S)?

4. Sulaimān asked on the jinn to bring him something from Sheba. What did he ask the Jinn to bring?

5. What is one of the names of prophet 'Isā (A) – the meaning of the name is 'the blessed one'?

6. What was the name of the Promised Land Mūsā wanted Israelites to occupy?

7. To which mountain did Mūsā go to receive Ten Commandments from Allāh?

8. When Mūsā and Khidir traveled together, what was the first incident Khidir did?

9. In which year Khadījah passed away?

10. In the Battle of Camel, who fought against whom?

11. What was the main form of transmission of Hadīth at the time of the Prophet (S)?

12. Against who did Goliath fight a dual that caused his death?

13. Which two prophets gave a judgment over a case involving sheep damaging crop of another man?

14. What did Sulaimān do with the throne of the queen of Sheba?

15. Who was the leader of the Israelites when Mūsā left for the mountain?

Answer:

1. Samuel	2. Bilqis	3. She was 40 years old
4. The throne	5. Masih	6. Canaan
7. Mount Sinai	8. Kidir made a hole in the boat	
9. 619 C.E. - known as the Year of Sorrow		10. 'Ā'ishah fought against 'Ali
11. Mostly orally	12. Dāwūd	13. Dāwūd and Sulaimān
14. He changed it	15. Hārūn	

Test Your Knowledge - 3

(All questions are based on the lessons taught in the book)

1. Who was known as the "Lady of the Light"?

2. In the Qur'ān who is known as Rūh-ul-Quddus?

3. What is the name of the angel who is the guard of hell?

4. Which country has the largest Muslim population?

5. Who were the parents of Hasan and Husayn?

6. The Christians believe in threefold representation of God. What is the term for that?

7. What is the Arabic term for Oneness of God?

8. What are the names of two angels who lived in ancient Babylon?

9. What is the name of the Jewish law books written by the Rabbis?

10. What is the name of the cave where Prophet (S) received the first revelation?

11. How long was the Prophet(S) married to Khadījah?

12. What was the name of the Khadījah's servant who went with Muhammad in Syria during trade?

13. What is Janntual Baqi?

14. What dynasty was formed after the name of Fātimah?

15. Who was affectionately called Umm Abi-ha?

Answer

1. Fātimah	2. Angel Jibril	3. Malik
4. Indonesia	5. 'Ali and Fātimah	6. Trinity
7. Tawhid	8. Hārūt and Mārūt	9. Talmud
10. Cave Hira	11. 25 years	12. Maysarah
13. Graveyard of many of the companions, it is is Madīnah		14. Fatimid Dynasty
15. Fātimah.		

Test Your Knowledge - 4
(All questions are based on the lessons taught in the book)

1. How long did it take the finish revelation of the Qur'ān?

2. Which compiler of Hadīth was born in Bukhara in Uzbekistan?

3. In which year Muhammad (S) and Khadījah got married?

4. What two things Allāh promised to Mūsā's mother when He told her to cast the baby in river?

5. What is the meaning of the word Tābi'īn?

6. Nūh wanted to save someone on the boat when flood started. Who did he want to save?

7. After how many years of marriage with Khadījah, Muhammad (S) received divine revelation?

8. What was the name of the divine book sent to prophet Dāwūd?

9. How many signs did Mūsā show to Fir'awn?

10. Which of the Prophet's wife had an incident with a necklace?

11. What is the first stage through which nafs passes?

12. What is the second stage through which nafs passes?

13. What is the third and final stage through which nafs passes?

14. What is the name of the angel who will blow the trumpet at the time of Awakening?

15. Allāh is the walī of the Muslims. What is the meaning of walī?

Answer:
1. 23 years   2. Imam Bukhārī   3. In 595 C.E.
4. He will return him and make him a prophet   5. The followers of Sahābah
6. His son   7. After 15 years   8. Zabūr or Psalms
9. Nine signs   10. 'Ā'ishah   11. Ammarah
12. Lawwamah   13. Mutma'innah   14. Israfil
15. Protecting friend

Outline of Curriculum – Grades 1, 2 and 3

Every year the curriculum begins with a few topics on Allāh, the Qur'ān, the Prophet (S), the Hadīth or Sunnah. In the early years the emphasis is given on the 5-pillars, but each year the emphasis increases. Every year history of some of the prophets is introduced in an age appropriate manner. Each year, several lessons are devoted to Islamic values to make the children grow up with good understanding of Islamic manners, values and morals. All the lessons are followed by homework.

Week	1st Grade	2nd Grade	3rd Grade
1	Allāh	Allāh the Creator	What does Allāh do
2	Islam	Blessings of Allāh	Some names of Allāh
3	Our Faith	The Qur'ān	Allāh : the Merciful
4	Muhammad (S)	Muhammad (S)	Allāh : the Judge
5	Qur'ān	Sunnah and Hadīth	We are Muslims
6	Exam is recommended in this week		
7	5 pillars of Islam	5 pillars of Islam	Other names of the Qur'ān
8	Shahādah	Shahādah	Hadith
9	Salāt and Wūdū	Salāt	Shahādah
10	Fasting	Sawm	Types of salāt
11	Zakah	Charity	Why to do salāt
12	Exam is recommended in this week		
13	Hajj	Hajj	Sawm
14	Saying bismillāh	Wūdū	Charity
15	Angels	Four khalīfas	Hajj
16	Shaitān	Ibrāhīm (A)	Prophet (S) in Makkah
17	Adam (A)	Ya'qūb (A) and Yūsuf (A)	Prophet (S) in Madinah
18	Nūh (A)	Mūsā (A) and Harun (A)	How Rasul (S) treated others
19	Exam is recommended in this week		
20	Ibrāhīm (A)	Yūnus (A)	Ismā'īl (A) and Ishāq (A)
21	Mūsā (A)	Angels	Dāwūd (A)
22	'Īsā (A)	Foods that we may eat	'Īsā (A)
23	Makkah and Madinah	Truthfulness	Being kind
24	Good manners	Kindness	Forgiveness
25	Kindness and sharing	Respect	Good deeds
26	Exam is recommended in this week		
27	Allāh rewards good works	Responsibility	Cleanliness
28	Respect	Obedience	Right Path
29	Forgiveness	Cleanliness	Muslim family
30	Love of Allāh	Honesty	Perseverance
31	Eid	Day of Judgment and Hereafter	Punctuality
32	Thanking Allāh	Muslims from different nations	Jinn
33	Exam is recommended in this week		

Outline of Curriculum – Grades 4, 5 and 6

By 5th grade a summarized biography of the Prophet (S) is completed with an understanding of events that shaped his life and early Islam. By 6th grade, the students will have studied the biography of most of the prominent prophets at least once. By now the students will have learned all the fundamental principles and all key concepts of Islam. Even if the students do not come back to weekend schools after 6th grade, still they will have gained significant age-appropriate knowledge about Islam.

Week	4th Grade	5th Grade	6th Grade
1	Rewards of Allāh	Allāh our sole Master	Attributes of Allāh
2	Discipline of Allāh	Why should we worship Allāh	Promise of Allāh
3	Some names of Allāh	Revelation of the Qur'ān	Objective of the Qur'ān
4	Books of Allāh	Characteristics of prophets	Compilation of the Qur'ān
5	Pre-Islamic Arabia	Battle of Badr	Previous Scriptures and the Qur'ān
6	Exam is recommended in this week		
7	The Year of the Elephant	Battle of Uhud	Importance of Shahādah
8	Early life of Muhammad (S)	Battle of Trench	Hadīth, compilation, narrators
9	Life before prophethood	Hudaibiyah Treaty	Nūh (A)
10	Receipt of prophethood	Conquest of Makkah	Talut, Jalut and Dāwūd (A)
11	Makkan period	Adam (A)	Dāwūd (A) and Sulaimān (A)
12	Exam is recommended in this week		
13	Pledges of Aqaba	Ibrāhīm (A) and his arguments	Sulaimān (A) and Queen of Saba
14	Hijrat to Madinah	Ibrāhīm (A) and idols	Mūsā (A) and Fir'awn
15	Madīnan period	Luqmān (A) and his teachings	Israelites after their rescue
16	Victory of Makkah	Yūsuf (A) – Childhood and life in Aziz's home	Mūsā (A) and Khidir
17	Abū Bakr (R)	Yūsuf (A) – life in prison and his dream interpretation	'Isā (A) and Maryam (ra)
18	'Umar al-Khattāb (R)	Yūsuf (A) - dream fulfills	Khadījah (ra)
19	Exam is recommended in this week		
20	'Uthmān ibn 'Affan (R)	Ayyūb (A)	'A'ishah (ra)
21	'Ali Ibn Abu Tālib (R)	Zakariyyāh (A) and Yahyā (A)	Fātimah (ra)
22	Compilers of Hadīth	Maryam	Awakening
23	Shaitān's mode of action	Major Masjid in the world	Rūh and Nafs
24	Hūd (A)	Upholding truth	Angel and Jinn
25	Sālih (A)	Responsibility and punctuality	Shaitān's strategy
26	Exam is recommended in this week		
27	Mūsā (A)	My mind, my body	Taqwā
28	Sulaimān (A)	Kindness and forgiveness	My friend is Muslim now
29	Truthfulness	Middle Path	Friendship with others / with opposite gender
30	Perseverance	Significance of salāt	Reading salāt vs performing salāt
31	Day of Judgment	Significance of fasting	Muslims around the world
32	'Eid and its significance	Zakāt and sadaqah - significance	People of other faith
33	Exam is recommended in this week		

Outline of Curriculum – Grades 7, 8 and 9

Application of knowledge is gradually emphasized through carefully selected topics. Details about some of the prophets are introduced to highlight the abiding moral in their lives. In 8th grade several battles and early Muslims' struggle are discussed in detail. Depth and emphasis in the lessons require increased attention from the students. Age appropriate moral lessons e.g. gossip, friendship, peer pressure, dating, indecency, enjoining good and forbidding evil, etc. are covered.

Week	7th Grade	8th Grade	9th Grade
1	Why Islam, what is Islam	Divine Names	Signs of Allāh in nature
2	The Qur'ān - other names	Objective of the Qur'ān	Ponder over the Qur'ān
3	Seeking forgiveness of Allāh - Istighfar	Hadīth	Preservation and compilation of the Qur'ān
4	Allāh: Angry or Kind	Madhhab	Ibadat - some easy ways to do it
5	Islamic Greetings	Hope, hopefulness, hopelessness	Why human being are superior
6	Exam is recommended in this week		
7	Adam (A)	Trial	Is Islam a violent religion
8	'Ad and Thamūd	Friends and friendship	Peer pressure
9	Stories of Ibrāhīm (A)-I	Friendship with Non-Muslims	Choices we make
10	Stories of Ibrāhīm (A) -II	Dating in Islam	Dating in Islam
11	Sacrifice of Ibrāhīm (A)	Duties towards Parents	Alcohol and gambling
12	Exam is recommended in this week		
13	Lūt (A)	Islam for middle school student	Permitted and prohibited food
14	Yūsuf (A)- Story of overcoming temptation	Battle of Badr	Food of the People of the Book
15	Dwellers of Cave	Battle of Uhud	Khadījah (ra)
16	Dhul Qurnain	Banu Qaynuka	Prophet's multiple marriages
17	Abū Sufyān	Banu Nadir	Marriage with Zainab (ra)
18	Khālid Ibn Walīd (R)	Battle of Khandaq	The Prophet - a great army general
19	Exam is recommended in this week		
20	How to achieve success	Banu Qurayzah	God's chosen people
21	Character of the prophets	Surah Al-Ahzāb on the Battle of Khandaq	Mūsā's personality
22	Prophet's marriages	Hudaibiyah Treaty	Prophecy of Muhammad(S) in Bible
23	Purification	Tabūk Expedition	Shī'ah Muslims
24	Permitted and prohibited	Farewell Pilgrimage	Muslims in North America
25	Lailatul Qadr	Performance of Hajj	Life cycle of truth
26	Exam is recommended in this week		
27	Fasting in Ramadan	Paradise and Hell	How Ramadan makes us better
28	My family is Muslim now	Finality of Prophethood	Indecency
29	Amr bil ma'rūf	Origin and history of Shī'ah	Allegations against the Prophet (S)
30	Guard your tongue	Ummayad Dynasty	Family values
31	Lessons from past civilizations	Abbasid Dynasty	Shariah
32	Science in the Qur'ān	Permitted and prohibited food	Justice in Islam
33	Exam is recommended in this week		

Outline of Curriculum – Grades 10, 11 and 12

In 10th, 11th and 12th grades, the topics increasingly prepare the youths to tune their young-adult life. More serious issues are introduced that have real life implications. Application of knowledge continues to be emphasized. Age appropriate moral lessons like righteousness in Islam, marriage, dowry issues, divorce process, music in Islam, jihād etc. are introduced.

Week	10th Grade	11th Grade	12th Grade
1	History of Allāh	"Discovering" God	Our God, their God
2	An analysis of Fātiha	Kalam of Allāh	Loving Allāh
3	Fātiha vs. Lord's Prayer	Precedence of mercy in Allāh	Literal interpretation of the Qur'ān
4	Muhkam Mutashabihat verses	Importance of the Qur'ān in life	Management 101 - from the Prophet's life
5	Being Khalifa on earth	Succession to Muhammad (S)	Apostasy
6	Exam is recommended in this week		
7	10 Companions - Ashara Mubashirin	Victory comes from apparent setback	Husband and wife - garment for each other
8	The Bible and the Qur'ān	Accountability	Dowry process
9	Adam and Eve in the Garden	Righteousness in Islam	Divorce process
10	Natural calamities	10 years of life changing foundation	Lian verses
11	Racism in Islam	Light upon the Light	Hijab verses
12	Exam is recommended in this week		
13	Superstition	Ruh, Nafs, Spirit, Bodies	Marital relations of the Prophet (S)
14	Al-Asr - timing of the Day	Responsibilities in married life	Men are head of household
15	Position of women in Islam	Divorce	Flogging an adulterer
16	Marriage with Non-Muslims	Balancing faith amid diversity	Why two women witness
17	Distinctive females in Qur'ān	Importance of keeping the "trust"	Hur in Heaven
18	Women's rights in Islam	Music in Islam	Is Islam a violent religion
19	Exam is recommended in this week		
20	Establishing salāt- Institutionalize it	Fitra - Innate human nature	Jihād verses
21	Goodly loan	Heedlessness in human being	Hajj - understanding the significance
22	Fiqh	Importance of tolerance	"Beating thy wife"
23	Death	Guidance and misguidance	"Part time Muslim"
24	Turmoil in early Islam	Stages of life and death	Muslim youths in the US
25	Public finance in early Islam	This world and next world	MSA - An introduction
26	Exam is recommended in this week		
27	Business ethics	How to enjoy life Islamic way	Islamophobia - how to deal with it
28	Balance in life	Wrongdoings - how to identify and avoid them	Future Muslims
29	Islam in America	How to pray Janaza prayer	Independent project
30	Islam in India	Understanding Judaism	Independent project
31	Islam in Spain	Judaism, Christianity and Islam	Independent project
32	Islam in Turkey	Dependence, independence	Independent project
33	Exam is recommended in this week		

Other useful books from weekend**Learning**

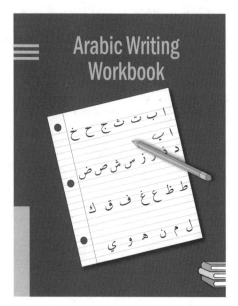

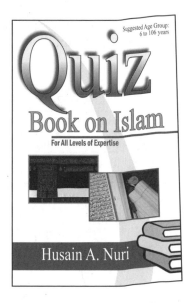

Arabic Writing Workbook

96 pages

Teach students how to write Arabic with easy to follow instructions. Practice alphabets are given in shaded and dotted form, followed by blank lines to polish writing skills. Plenty of pages for year long practice writing.

21 Du'ā for Children: Supplications from Al-Qur'ān

By Mansur Ahmad

28 pages

Allāh wants us to always make du'ā to Him for everything. The finest du'ā are those taught by Allāh in the Qur'ān. Use this booklet to teach 21 finest du'ā and many more. Give one copy to each student in your school. It is a life long companion and a great learning tool.

Quiz Book on Islam for All Levels of Expertise

By Husain A. Nuri

140 pages

Written by Quiz Master of an Interstate Quiz Bowl. The book is designed to boost the knowledge base of all students. Even adults will enjoy the book. The book has over 1,450 questions covering 89 different topics. The questions are divided into basic and advanced sections. Each page has about 15 - 17 questions. Many questions have explanatory answers. Turn to this book to quickly learn a lot about Islam.

These books and other useful titles are available from weekend**Learning** Publishers. Please visit the website for additional details. www.weekendlearning.com